# Bible Story

## CRAFTS & PROJECTS

# Children Love

**Group**

Loveland, Colorado

## Bible Story Crafts & Projects Children Love

Copyright © 1995 Group Publishing, Inc.

## Credits

Contributing Authors: Lorie Barnes, Carolyn Berge, Jacqui Dunham, Susan Grover, Lois Keffer, Susan Lingo, Gail Marsh, Lori Haynes Niles, and Beth Wolf.
Book Acquisitions Editor: Mike Nappa
Editor: Jody Brolsma
Senior Editor: Lois Keffer
Creative Products Director: Joani Schultz
Copy Editor: Amy Simpson
Art Director: Lisa Smith
Cover Art Director: Liz Howe
Computer Graphic Artist: Randy Kady
Cover Illustrator: Paula Becker
Illustrator: Sharon Holm
Production Manager: Gingar Kunkel

Bible story crafts and projects children love.
     p.   cm.
   ISBN 1-55945-698-1
   1. Bible crafts. 2. Christian education of children. I. Group Publishing.
BS613.B484 1995                        95-22445
268'.432--dc20                           CIP

10 9 8 7 6 5 4 3 2 1     04 03 02 01 00 99 98 97 96 95
Printed in the United States of America.

# Contents

# Introduction

*"In the beginning you made the earth, and your hands made
the skies" (Psalm 102:25).*

Take a look around you for countless examples of God's amazing creativity: giraffes casually nibbling leaves from the tiptop of a tree, tuxedoed penguins sliding across an icy glacier, a fiery sunset burning across an evening sky, and snowflakes daintily resting on the branches of an evergreen. But God's most spectacular creation is holding this book—you! God made humans in his image, complete with his creative and imaginative spirit.

Let's not forget this when we choose arts and crafts that teach the Bible to our children. It's easy to settle for the same repertoire of ideas we grew up with. Most of those crafts will have short lives hanging on the refrigerator, only to be tossed into the garbage can. What does that say about the value and meaning of the projects?

Wouldn't it be exciting to send your students home with something really meaningful? something they can use again? something that will remind them of the Bible story they've just learned? If you want your students to use their God-given creativity and imagination to make things with real meaning and value, then read on!

You'll find this book filled with unique art and craft ideas that will help reinforce Bible truths and stories for your elementary children. Many are take-home crafts, while others are larger cooperative projects meant to stay in your classroom. You'll find the supplies readily available at your local craft or hobby store.

Here are a few suggestions to make your craft times enjoyable and productive for everyone.

- **Try the craft ahead of time.** Although you'll find the instructions and diagrams in this book clear and helpful, there's nothing like experience to make you a confident leader. Doing the craft ahead of time will help you avoid any unexpected problems.
- **Know your students and their abilities.** Some projects are more difficult than others, particularly for younger children. Crafts that are too difficult leave children feeling frustrated and unmotivated. Set your children up for success by choosing crafts that are appropriate to their skills.
- **Allow for individual creativity.** Arts and crafts are a wonderful way for kids to express themselves. Avoid the temptation to judge one student's work as better or more acceptable than another's. Encourage all children in their efforts and celebrate their accomplishments.

You have in your hand the very best ideas from outstanding teachers all across the nation. So jump right in! Remember: God has given all of us the gifts of creativity and imagination. Put those gifts to good use in your craft times and watch with delight as the Bible comes to life for kids!

# The Old Testament

# Creation

**T**he first two chapters of Genesis paint a vivid picture of how God created our world and everything in it. We can only stand in awe as God's love, power, and creativity burst forth, transforming a formless void into light, oceans, mountains, animals, and people. Use the ideas in this section to help children focus on God's creative power as they learn to appreciate God's awesome creation and their part in it.

**1.** Genesis 1 and 2 show the wonder and diversity of God's creation. Use Idea 1, "Paper Petals," to help kids celebrate the creativity and beauty of God's world.

**2.** When God placed the first people in the Garden of Eden, he gave them specific instructions to care for their surroundings (Genesis 1:28-29). Idea 2, "Home Tweet Home," gives kids the opportunity to follow God's instructions. Making a birdhouse is a practical way for young students to care for God's creation.

**3.** The Garden of Eden offered Adam and Eve first-class accommodations. God provided in abundance for their every need (Genesis 1:29-30). Use Idea 3, "Edible Landscapes," to remind kids of the wealth and variety of good foods God provides for their enjoyment.

**4.** From the elephant's huge ears to the mouse's tiny whiskers, we see the breadth of God's imaginative, creative power. Idea 4, "Creation Costumes," will allow kids to disguise themselves as some of God's other creatures.

# 1. Paper Petals

*Children will make tissue paper flowers to brighten the room.*

**Theme:** God made a beautiful world for us.

**Scripture Spotlight 1:** "The Lord God planted a garden in the east, in a place called Eden, and put the man he had formed into it" (Genesis 2:8).

**Scripture Spotlight 2:** "Lord, you have made many things; with your wisdom you made them all" (Psalm 104:24a).

**Collect:** Tissue paper, scissors, a hole punch, green chenille wire, and bowls of food coloring and water

## Here's What to Do:

Before class, cut several 4-inch circles from tissue paper. An easy way to do this is to stack five squares together, fold them into quarters, then round the outer edges.

Give kids eight paper circles apiece and instruct them to stack these together. Show kids how to fold the circles into quarters and cut the outer edges into petal shapes. Have kids unfold the circles and use a hole punch to poke two holes in the center. The holes should be about ¼ inch apart. Demonstrate how to thread the chenille wire through the holes and pull the ends even underneath the paper. Have kids gently pinch their paper up and away from the wire. Twist the wire together to form one single "stem."

Demonstrate how to open the petals of the flower and spread them out carefully. Have kids dip just the tips of the petals in a bowl of food coloring and water. Set the flowers in a sunny place to dry.

## For Further Fun:
● Have kids make several flowers, then arrange them in a vase or planter. Set your bouquet in the sanctuary for others to enjoy!

● Bend a wire coat hanger into the shape of a heart or a cross. Allow kids to weave the stems of their flowers onto the wire frame to make a colorful paper topiary.

# 2. Home Tweet Home

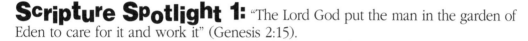

*Help kids make birdhouses for small birds.*

**Theme:** God wants us to care for his creation.

**Scripture Spotlight 1:** "The Lord God put the man in the garden of Eden to care for it and work it" (Genesis 2:15).

**Scripture Spotlight 2:** "You put [people] in charge of everything you made" (Psalm 8:6a).

**Collect:** Small craft sticks (37 for each student), a saw, ¼-inch plywood or cork, wood glue, wax paper, and clear acrylic sealer

## Here's What to Do:
Before class, cut the plywood or cork into equilateral triangles measuring 4 inches on each side. Also, cut a 1½-inch square in half of the triangles to serve as the entrances for the birdhouses. Each child will need two triangles, one with the entrance cut out.

Have kids sit at a table with all materials within easy reach. Give children squares of wax paper to work on. Help students with each of the following steps, making sure that sticks are securely glued as directed.

Say: **Use two craft sticks to make the number 11 on your wax paper. The sticks should be about three inches apart. Now glue 10 sticks on top of these, facing the other way, with sides touching. These will form the birdhouse floor.**

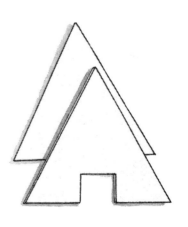

When kids have finished this step, say: **Now spread wood glue on the bottom edges of both triangle pieces and set them in place to form the front and back walls. Each stick of the floor should be securely glued to these walls.** (Note: If the front wall is positioned as shown, the roof will form an overhang, offering more protection from wind and rain.)

Have kids hold the front and back walls securely to the craft sticks for 90 seconds. If you want the glue to dry quickly, you can use hot glue instead. Have an adult helper apply the hot glue, and warn children to keep their fingers far away from the hot glue and the glue gun. Let the glue dry a bit before the next step. When everyone has finished, say: **Next, use your finger to spread glue on the sloped edges of the triangles. Beginning at the bottom, lay sticks in place to form the sides of**

the roof. Roofing sticks should be glued to each other as well as to the front and back walls. Be sure not to use too much glue or this won't dry properly!

Help kids make their craft sticks fit together tightly. When kids have finished both walls of their birdhouses, say: **Finally, glue two sticks together and glue them to the middle of the cut-out door for a perch.**

Set the birdhouses aside to dry. After about 20 minutes, have an adult supervise while kids apply two or three coats of clear acrylic sealer to weatherproof the birdhouses.

## For Further Fun:

● Make extra birdhouses to hang in trees near your church. Let kids scatter seeds, bread crumbs, or grain for their "tenants."

● Have kids smear peanut butter on pine cones then roll the pine cones in birdseed. Hang these bird feeders near your birdhouses or near classroom windows so kids can watch the birds enjoying their special treat.

# 3. Edible Landscapes

*Kids will have fun making—and eating—this project!*

**Theme:** God made good food for our enjoyment.

**Scripture Spotlight 1:** "God said, 'Look, I have given...food for you'" (Genesis 1:29).

**Scripture Spotlight 2:** "All living things look to you for food, and you give it to them at the right time" (Psalm 145:15).

**Collect:** Sturdy paper plates and your choice of colorful foods such as broccoli, carrots, celery, cauliflower, blue finger gelatin, lettuce, coconut, and mini muffins

## Here's What to Do:

Set food items out on a table and give each child a sturdy paper plate. Invite children to make landscapes with the food. Let children choose foods they like to eat and arrange them to form landscapes. Blue finger gelatin can become a lake or river, cauliflower and broccoli can make trees and bushes, and coconut can become snow on top of a mini muffin mountain. Encourage kids to use their imagination and creativity to make delicious and attractive pictures. Be sure everyone displays his or her landscape before eating it!

## For Further Fun:

● Let children enjoy their edible landscapes in small groups. Encourage them to name good and beautiful things in God's creation as they eat their landscape creations.

● Have kids create an enormous landscape on a large piece of cardboard. Perhaps it can resemble a park near your church.

# 4. Creation Costumes

*Children will transform themselves into new creations.*

**Theme:** God's creation praises him.

**Scripture Spotlight 1:** "God looked at everything he had made, and it was very good" (Genesis 1:31a).

**Scripture Spotlight 2:** "Let everything that breathes praise the Lord" (Psalm 150:6a).

**Collect:** Your choice of materials such as boxes (all sizes), balloons, paper plates, yarn, construction paper, aluminum foil, tape, markers, chenille wire, crayons, scissors, and crepe paper streamers

# Here's What to Do:

Set out the materials you've gathered, then form pairs. Tell kids to use the materials to help their partners make creation costumes that will transform them into another one of God's creations. For example, one child might tape purple balloons all over himself and be transformed into a bunch of grapes. Another student might wear a box she's designed to look like a tiger. Someone else might decorate a paper plate for a flower mask.

Give just a few ideas, then encourage kids to dream up their own designs.

# For Further Fun:

● Consider using the creation costumes to present the story of creation to another class.

● Let everyone participate in a creation parade so other classes and adults can see the kids' creations.

# The Great Flood

*Adam and Eve's sin spoiled God's perfect creation. Soon the world was so full of wickedness that God was sorry he'd ever made human beings (Genesis 6:6). God decided to cleanse the earth of evil by sending a cataclysmic flood. However, a man named Noah had found favor with God because he was good and honorable and he "walked with God" (Genesis 6:9). God chose to spare Noah, his family, and a pair of every animal that lived on the land or in the air (Genesis 6:18-21). Use the ideas in this section to show kids that God offers love and protection to all who obey him.*

**1.** When God saw how wicked people had become, he was sorry he had made them (Genesis 6:1-7). Noah was the only man who obeyed God and followed his commands (Genesis 6:8, 9). That's why God told Noah to build an ark that would save Noah's family and two of each kind of animal. Idea 1, "Ark Builders," will help kids see the benefits of obedience.

**2.** God loved the animals he'd created and wanted them to be a part of the new, clean world after The Flood. So he told Noah to take a pair of each animal with him on the ark. Idea 2, "Paper Cup Pets," will help kids create winsome animals of their own.

**3.** Just as God provided protection for Noah and his family, he provided safety for the animals (Genesis 7:9). Use Idea 3, "Two by Two," to remind kids that God cares for animals, too.

**4.** When Noah, his family, and the animals were safe inside the ark, God shut the door. Just as God had promised, the rain began and didn't end for 40 days and 40 nights. Every living thing on earth was destroyed (Genesis 7:12-24). Use Idea 4, "Raindrops Keep Falling," to help kids understand that God controls the wind and rain.

**5.** Finally the rain stopped and the ark rested on land. God had kept his word. Noah and his family and all the animals were safe (Genesis 8:1-14). God placed a rainbow in the sky as a sign of his promise that he would never again flood the entire earth. Use Idea 5, "God's Gift," to celebrate God's promises to those who love him.

# 1. Ark Builders

*Trios will work together to create a classroom ark.*

**Theme:** God wants us to obey him.

**Scripture Spotlight 1:** "Noah did everything that God commanded him" (Genesis 6:22).

**Scripture Spotlight 2:** "If you love me, you will obey my commands" (John 14:15).

**Collect:** Paper grocery sacks, newspaper or scrap paper, masking tape, and brown crayons

## Here's What to Do:

Form trios and give each trio several paper grocery sacks, brown crayons, and a stack of newspaper or scrap paper. Say: **We're going to make an ark from all these bags. To make a neat texture, crumple up your bags but don't rip them! Then uncrumple the bags and color them with the brown crayons.**

While trios are crumpling and coloring the bags, tell them to fill each bag with wadded-up newspapers or scrap paper. Show kids how to fold the top of a bag down twice to make a flat top then tape it shut.

As trios finish making their paper bag "building blocks," have them place the bags in the middle of the room then work together to form a rectangle to represent the ark. Kids can stack their building block bags on top of each other to make the ark about three blocks tall. The ark will be precarious (and fun!), so you may want older kids to oversee the stacking process, using masking tape to secure the bags.

## For Further Fun:

● Have kids form pairs and take turns carefully climbing "aboard" the ark. Kids can experience how crowded and exciting the ark must have been.

● While kids are building the ark, encourage them to make building noises, such as the pounding of hammers and the scraping of saws, to add realism to the construction process.

# 2. Paper Cup Pets

*Kids will create animals from Noah's floating zoo.*

**Theme:** God loves his creation.

**Scripture Spotlight 1:** "Also, you must bring into the boat two of every living thing, male and female" (Genesis 6:19a).

**Scripture Spotlight 2:** "Look at the birds in the air. They don't plant or harvest or store food in barns, but your heavenly Father feeds them" (Matthew 6:26a).

**Collect:** Paper cups, scissors, pencils, crayons, construction paper, felt, glue, and chenille wire

## Here's What to Do:

Give each child one paper cup and a pair of scissors. Show kids how to turn the cup upside down and, using a pencil, poke and enlarge two finger holes near the

rim. Have older children help younger ones who may have trouble with this step. Be sure kids can fit their fingers through the holes. Explain that kids' fingers will become the front legs for an animal.

Set out all other materials. Allow kids to cut ears, eyes, noses, or wings from the construction paper then work with the other materials to decorate their cups as they create their animals. Chenille wire can be used for tails or antennae, felt can become ears or fur, and crayons can add color and detail.

## For Further Fun:

● Have kids create partners for their paper cup pets then march all of the pairs of animals into a box or toy boat.

● Allow kids to create human puppets the same way. Kids may make Noah, his wife, and their family to join the animals on the ark!

# 3. Two by Two

*Pairs will make wearable art.*

**Theme:** We can count on God to keep us safe.

**Scripture Spotlight 1:** "They went into the boat in groups of two...just as God had commanded Noah" (Genesis 7:9).

**Scripture Spotlight 2:** "We know that those who are God's children do not continue to sin. The Son of God keeps them safe, and the Evil One cannot touch them" (1 John 5:18).

**Collect:** Large, plain animal crackers; clear fingernail polish; wiggly eyes; pin backs; a glue gun; wax paper or vinyl place mats; acrylic paints; and permanent markers

## Here's What to Do:

Have kids form pairs, then give each pair a handful of animal crackers and a sheet of wax paper or a vinyl place mat. Allow kids to choose their favorite animal crackers and paint the front of each with a coat of clear fingernail polish. Before the polish dries, have kids add wiggly eyes to the front of the crackers, where the animals' eyes would be. Children may choose to use permanent markers or acrylic paints to decorate their animals to look like carousel or real animals. When the polish has dried, have children turn the crackers over, paint the undersides, and glue on pin backs. When the glue dries, have partners attach the pins to each other's clothes.

## For Further Fun:

● Prerecord animal sounds and play them while kids work. Have kids try to identify each sound.

● Have each child gather with others who created a pin from the same animal. Students can read the story of Noah in Genesis 6–8 and talk about how God protects them today.

# 4. Raindrops Keep Falling

*Kids will create paintings awash with color and sparkle.*

**Theme:** Even the winds and rain obey God.

**Scripture Spotlight 1:** "The underground springs split open, and the clouds in the sky poured out rain. The rain fell on the earth for forty days and forty nights" (Genesis 7:11b,12).

**Scripture Spotlight 2:** "The wind and the waves obey him" (Matthew 8:27b).

**Collect:** Crayons, watercolor paper, blue watercolor paint, paintbrushes, full salt shakers, and newspaper

## Here's What to Do:

Assemble three stations, each in a different area of the room. Lay down newspaper and provide these materials at the following stations:

Crayon Creators—crayons and watercolor paper

Watercolor Washers—blue watercolor paint and paintbrushes

Salty Sprinklers—several full salt shakers

Have kids start at the Crayon Creators station and create pictures of what Noah's ark might have looked like. Be sure they press down firmly with the crayons. When kids finish their pictures, send them to the Watercolor Washers area, where they can brush watercolor paint over their crayon pictures. Then have kids move to the Salty Sprinklers area, and show them how to sprinkle salt over the wet pictures. When the salt and water dry, the pictures will sparkle!

## For Further Fun:

● Combine 1 cup of tempera paint with ½ cup of white corn syrup. Have kids use this mixture to create more rain pictures. The paint shines even after it's dry!

● Mix ½ cup of sugar with ⅓ cup of water to form a thick liquid. Instead of having kids sprinkle salt over the pictures, have them brush the pictures with the sugar water. When the water dries, the sugar crystals will sparkle.

# 5. God's Gift

*Kids will create metallic rainbow streamers.*

**Theme:** God's promises are fulfilled.

**Scripture Spotlight 1:** "Floods will never again destroy all life on the earth" (Genesis 9:15b).

**Scripture Spotlight 2:** "He is a faithful God who does no wrong, who is right and fair" (Deuteronomy 32:4b).

**Collect:** Plastic straws, staplers, and 3-foot (or longer) lengths of metallic streamers in rainbow colors

## Here's What to Do:

Give each student five metallic streamers and a plastic straw. Have kids staple the streamers to the straws anyway they'd like. Students may want to staple all of the streamers to one end, place them at both ends, or space them out along the straws. Show kids how to wave the streamers to make rainbows.

## For Further Fun:

● Have kids make two or three streamers each. March into church, singing a praise song and waving streamers. As kids march, have them give extra streamers away to adults as they invite them to join the celebration.

● Form teams and have fun with rainbow relays. See if kids can run through an obstacle course without letting go of their streamers.

# Moses and the Exodus

**T**he Exodus and the wilderness wanderings were incredible events in Israel's history. Thousands of Hebrew people left the country where they'd been slaves for 430 years (Exodus 12:40-41), then they trudged through the desert for over 40 years before finally coming to the land God had promised to them. During that time God taught them to trust him for food, protection, and guidance. God gave them the laws and principles that would make them his own people. Use these ideas to help children focus on God's powerful protection and care.

**1.** Moses' life began on an exciting note! His mother placed him in a tar-covered basket made of river reeds and gently set him among the plants along the shore of a river (Exodus 2:3). Use Idea 1, "Tiny Baskets," to show children that God has a plan for them, too, and that God will keep them safe.

**2.** Moses warned Pharaoh that unless he freed the Israelites, God would send disastrous plagues on Egypt. The eighth of these plagues was an enormous swarm of locusts that destroyed the Egyptian crops. Idea 2, "Bouncy Bugs," will remind kids that God uses his power to help his people.

**3.** When Pharaoh finally told the Israelites to leave Egypt, there was no time for lengthy farewells. So the Israelites quickly packed all of their animals and as many possessions as they could gather. They hurriedly baked dough without yeast, creating the tradition of celebrating Passover with matzo bread. Use Idea 3, "Quick Bread," to teach children to follow instructions as the Israelites did.

**4.** Moses wasn't sure he was the one to lead the Israelites to the Promised Land. He doubted his leadership abilities and speaking skills in light of such an enormous task (Exodus 3–4). But God proved that it would be divine power, not Moses' power, that would deliver the Israelites from the hand of Pharaoh. Idea 3, "Sneaky Snake," will help kids discover that God's power can help them do great things.

**5.** After the Israelites had journeyed for many days, God taught them how to be his people. He gave them the Ten Commandments to show them how to respect God and how to treat each other (Exodus 20:1-17). The Israelites agreed to the rules and entered into a solemn covenant with God. God's rules are important for us, too. Use Idea 5, "Hidden in Your Heart," to remind kids that following God's rules will help them lead safe and happy lives.

# 1. Tiny Baskets

*Help children weave baskets to remind them of Moses' "baby" basket.*

**Theme:** God has a plan for us.

**Scripture Spotlight 1:** "But after three months she was not able to hide the baby any longer, so she got a basket and covered it with tar so that it would float. She put the baby in the basket. Then she put the basket among the tall stalks of grass at the edge of the Nile River" (Exodus 2:3).

**Scripture Spotlight 2:** " 'I say this because I know what I am planning for you,' says the Lord. 'I have good plans for you, not plans to hurt you' " (Jeremiah 29:11a).

**Collect:** Sticks and twigs, floral moss, glue, raffia, cereal boxes, and scissors

## Here's What to Do:

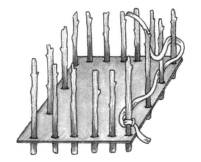

Unfold the cereal boxes and cut apart the front and back panels. Cut creative shapes out of the cardboard, being sure to make them about 4 inches wide. You'll need one cardboard shape for each student, as this will be the bottom of the basket.

Take kids outside and help them find several sticks of about the same length. You may want to have craft sticks on hand in case students have trouble finding enough natural sticks. When kids have found large handfuls of sticks, have them use the tip of a pair of scissors to poke small holes about one inch apart around their cardboard shapes. These holes should be at least ½ inch inside the edge of the cardboard.

Then have kids create the sides of the baskets by poking the sticks through the holes. No more than ¼ inch of the sticks should come through the bottom of the cardboard. Have kids put drops of glue where the sticks poke through to hold them in place. Set the baskets in the sun for a minute to let the glue dry. When the glue is dry, show children how to weave raffia in and out through the sticks. Start at the cardboard base and weave around the basket up to the top of the sticks. Have kids tie off the raffia when they reach the top and tuck the ends into the weaving.

When kids are finished weaving, have them glue the floral moss to the bottom of the baskets.

## For Further Fun:

● Have children take their baskets outside and fill them with natural items that remind them of God's care.

● Have children write notes of encouragement to each other and deliver them to each other's baskets.

# 2. Bouncy Bugs

*Kids will make bugs like the locusts God sent.*

**Theme:** God uses his power to help us.

**Scripture Spotlight 1:** "The Lord told Moses, 'Raise your hand over the land of Egypt, and the locusts will come. They will spread all over the land of Egypt and will eat all the plants...' " (Exodus 10:12).

**Scripture Spotlight 2:** "This was so that your faith would be in God's power and not in human wisdom" (1 Corinthians 2:5).

**Collect:** Colored yarn, scissors, chenille wire, florists wire, and wiggly eyes

## Here's What to Do:

Give each child at least 6 feet of colored yarn. Have each child hold one hand horizontally so the thumb is on top and the palm is facing in. Show kids how to wrap the yarn around their hands, keeping their fingers together.

The more yarn kids can use, the puffier their bugs will be. When students reach the end of their yarn, help them carefully pull the wound yarn off their hands and pinch it in the middle to form figure eights. Then distribute 5-inch sections of yarn and show students how to tie them around the middle of their bundles. Have kids cut off the leftover strands.

Distribute 9-inch lengths of florists wire and show kids how to wrap one end of the wire around their knots a few times. When kids have secured one end of the florists wire to the yarn, have them cut the looped ends of their figure eights and fluff up the loose strands of yarn. Allow kids to decorate the bugs using wiggly eyes and chenille wire. The bugs will bounce on the wire stems!

## For Further Fun:

● When you tell the story of the plague of locusts, have kids dart back and forth across the room holding their bugs and saying "bzzz."

● Have kids make "bug buddies" (bugs without stems) to attach to their shoelaces.

**Teacher Tip:**
Be sure kids keep the yarn fairly loose. If they wrap it too tightly, it could cut off the circulation in their fingers.

# 3. Quick Bread

*Kids will make and eat 18-minute matzo bread just like Jewish people make today.*

**Theme:** Always be ready to obey God.

**Scripture Spotlight 1:** "The Israelites used the dough they had brought out of Egypt to bake loaves of bread without yeast. The dough had no yeast in it, because they had been rushed out of Egypt and had no time to get food ready for their trip" (Exodus 12:39).

**Scripture Spotlight 2:** "Be dressed, ready for service, and have your lamps shining" (Luke 12:35).

**Collect:** Flour, water, mixing bowls, measuring cups, rolling pins, greased baking sheets, forks, a kitchen timer, and napkins

## Here's What to Do:

Explain that the Israelites had to leave Egypt so quickly that they didn't have time to finish making their bread. They baked it without yeast, so they had flat bread.

Say: **When Jewish people make this kind of bread for the Passover feast, they make it in less than 18 minutes to remember how quickly their ancestors had to leave Egypt. Let's make the same kind of bread in 18 minutes or less.**

This recipe will make enough matzo bread for eight children. If you have more than eight children, set up two groups and make two batches.

Before you begin timing, allow a volunteer to turn the oven to 450 degrees and make sure all children have washed their hands well. Have one child measure 3 cups of flour into a mixing bowl while another child measures 1½ cups of water into another bowl. Choose one or two kids who will mix the dough later. Give everyone else rolling pins and forks and explain that they'll be rollers and pokers.

Set the kitchen timer for 18 minutes and begin. Pour the water into the flour and have the mixers mix the dough with their hands. Add flour as needed so that the dough is pliable—neither crumbly nor sticky. When the dough is mixed, have kids divide it into eight sections and give one section to each of the rollers. Have them roll the dough out until it's thin, about ⅟₁₆ to ⅛ of an inch thick. Carefully place the rolled-out dough on the greased baking sheets and have the children use their forks to prick holes in the dough.

Put the baking sheets in the oven and bake for 10 to 12 minutes. When the matzo is done, have children hurriedly wrap it in napkins and take it outside to eat.

### For Further Fun:
● Allow kids to prick their initials in the dough.
● Have kids take their matzo to another class. Children may tell the story of the Exodus while they share their bread.

# 4. Sneaky Snake
*Kids will create creepy crawlers!*

**Theme:** God's power helps us do great things.

**Scripture Spotlight 1:** "When Moses reached out and took hold of the snake, it again became a stick in his hand. The Lord said, 'This is so that the Israelites will believe that the Lord appeared to you' " (Exodus 4:4b-5a).

**Scripture Spotlight 2:** "My teaching and preaching were not with words of human wisdom that persuade people but with proof of the power that the Spirit gives. This was so that your faith would be in God's power and not in human wisdom" (1 Corinthians 2:4-5).

**Collect:** ¼ yard of colorful cotton fabric per child, scissors, pencils, newsprint, permanent markers or fabric paint, sand or uncooked rice, needles and thread, and a funnel

## Here's What to Do:
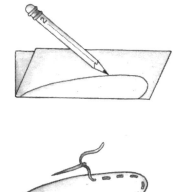

Form pairs and instruct partners to help each other as they make the craft. Distribute colorful cotton fabric, scissors, a needle, and thread to each student. Instruct kids to fold their fabric in half lengthwise. While one partner holds his or her folded fabric, have the other use a pencil to draw a long rounded shape similar to the one in the margin. You may want to draw this design on a chalkboard or sheet of newsprint so kids can use it as a guideline. After they've drawn the rounded figure, have one partner hold the fabric while the other cuts along the pencil line. Have partners switch roles so they each get to cut their own fabric.

Instruct kids to open the fabric, lay it on newsprint, and draw snakelike designs on it with fabric paint or markers. Remind kids that the top of the snake is where the fabric was folded. Allow the snakes to dry in a sunny place.

When the fabric is dry, have kids fold the fabric with the painted side facing in. Show students how to sew the fabric together, leaving a ½-inch seam. Partners can help each other with this step. Be sure kids leave an opening at the tail end. Show students how to turn the snake inside out through this hole so the painted design is on the outside.

Lead children outside and have one partner hold his or her snake with the open end up while the other partner holds a funnel inside the hole. Pour sand or uncooked rice into the funnel until each snake is filled. Then have partners help each other sew up the tails.

## For Further Fun:

● Explain that kids can use the snakes to stop drafts by laying them along the bases of doors. Curled up, the snakes make good doorstops, too!

● Kids can stuff the snakes with fiberfill to make stuffed animals for their rooms.

**Teacher Tip:**
You may want to ask an adult helper to sew the seams quickly on a sewing machine.

# 5. Hidden in Your Heart

*Kids will make faded pictures as reminders to honor God's commandments.*

## Theme: God's rules are important.

## Scripture Spotlight 1: "So now if you obey me and keep my agreement, you will be my own possession, chosen from all nations. Even though the whole earth is mine, you will be my kingdom of priests and a holy nation" (Exodus 19:5-6a).

## Scripture Spotlight 2: "I have taken your words to heart so I would not sin against you" (Psalm 119:11).

## Collect: Bibles, brightly colored construction paper, scissors, transparent tape, pencils, a spray bottle filled with two parts bleach and one part water, paint smocks or shirts, and paint pens or glitter markers

## Here's What to Do:

Give each child two pieces of brightly colored construction paper. Stick with the darker colors—yellow, pink, and light blue won't work well for this activity.

Have children look up Exodus 20:1-17 and write one of the Ten Commandments in the middle of their colored paper. Then have kids each cut a large heart from another sheet of construction paper. Help children make small transparent tape rolls then gently tape their paper hearts over the written commandments. The hearts must completely cover the commandments.

Take the pictures outside and allow kids to spray them with the bleach and water solution. Be sure kids are wearing paint smocks or shirts and are spraying away from all other students. Leave the papers in the sun for a minute or two. Kids will enjoy watching the paper fade.

When the paper is dry, allow kids to remove the hearts, being careful not to tear the paper. The sun and bleach will have faded all areas of the paper that were exposed.

Have kids write Psalm 119:11 at the top of the pictures with paint pens or glitter markers.

## For Further Fun:

● Have each child make a page for a different commandment. Put these together in a book of God's commands.

# Joshua

**J**oshua's escapades could be the basis for an action-packed adventure movie. His story, as told in Joshua 1–10 and concluding with Joshua 24, is filled with courageous episodes, unusual battles, surprise attacks, and spies galore. Overall, it's a story of Joshua's unfailing trust, dependence, and loyalty to God in what would seem to most of us to be a "mission impossible." Use the ideas in this section to help children focus on and learn from Joshua's exciting life.

**1.** The Israelites who'd been led out of Egypt by Moses had died in the desert because they had failed to follow God. Now *their* children, under Joshua's leadership, were ready to cross the Jordan River into Canaan. God showed them he was in charge by holding back the waters of the Jordan River (Joshua 3). Use Idea 1, "A New Perspective," to show that God can do anything!

**2.** After parting the Jordan River, God commanded Joshua and his people to never forget the event (Joshua 4). One representative from each of the 12 tribes was to choose a rock from the riverbed to use in building a memorial. Use Idea 2, "Monumental Love," to remind kids that like Joshua's people, they are children in God's family.

**3.** The Israelites faced a formidable challenge: to conquer all of the cities of Canaan. They started with the famous battle of Jericho. Use Idea 3, "And They All Came Tumbling Down," to help children experience the Bible story and to remind them of God's awesome power.

**4.** One of the strongest Canaanite cities was the city of Gibeon, which was ruled by a fearless king. Joshua met their challenge with a surprise attack. God miraculously stopped the sun and the moon in the sky until the battle was over and Joshua was safely back at the base camp. Use Idea 4, "When Time Stood Still," to help children imagine a day when the sun stopped moving.

**5.** As Joshua prepared to die, he reminded the Israelites that in the future they would have to make choices about whom they would serve. He also reminded them that choices have consequences, good and bad. Use Idea 5, "A Household of Strength," to help children realize they can make choices that honor God.

# 1. A New Perspective

*Pairs will work to create a perspective painting of the Israelites crossing the Jordan River.*

**Theme:** God is mighty.

**Scripture Spotlight 1:** "The priests carried the Ark of the Agreement with the Lord to the middle of the river and stood there on dry ground. They waited there while all the people of Israel walked across the Jordan River on dry land" (Joshua 3:17).

**Scripture Spotlight 2:** "And you will know that God's power is very great for us who believe. That power is the same as the great strength God used to raise Christ from the dead and put him at his right side in the heavenly world" (Ephesians 1:19-20).

**Collect:** For each pair of students: two plastic straws, two 8-inch squares cut from brown paper grocery sacks, 2 to 3 tablespoons of blue tempera paint thinned with water, a spoon, one-half of a plastic foam meat tray, markers, and transparent tape (optional: pieces of gold foil)

# Here's What to Do:

Before this activity, cut 8-inch squares from brown paper grocery sacks. If you have older children, allow them to help with the cutting.

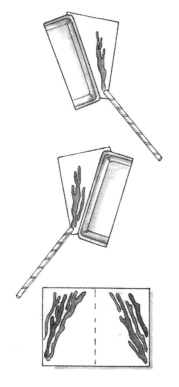

Have each student find a friend to work with. Be sure each pair has two plastic straws, two 8-inch squares of paper, approximately 2 tablespoons of thinned blue tempera paint to share, a spoon, and one-half of a plastic foam meat tray. Explain that kids will be using the straws to blow paint from one corner of their papers to the other. Have one partner place a spoonful of paint on the lower right-hand corner of his or her paper. While he or she blows the paint to the opposite corner, have the other partner set the plastic foam meat tray across the paper diagonally to keep the paint from getting on the other half of the paper.

When the paint touches the upper left-hand corner, have partners work together to fill in the upper right-hand corner by blowing more paint. Then have the other partner repeat this process, blowing paint from the lower *left* corner to the upper *right* corner of his or her paper.

When pairs have finished their paint blowing, show them how to put the paintings together so the unpainted sections form a large triangle in the middle. Tell children they'll be making a *perspective* drawing of the Israelites crossing the Jordan River, so it will seem that the figures in the picture are vanishing in the distance. To create this illusion, kids will need to make things at the bottom of the page larger than things at the top.

Show kids how to draw a trail of Israelites walking up the "dry" path in the middle of each picture. Partners may use the pieces of gold foil to make an ark as well.

# For Further Fun:

● Use this same method to create a wall mural of the parting of the Jordan River. Form two groups and have one group blow the paint while the other group diverts it with the meat trays. Then have groups switch roles. Instruct kids to work together to draw the Israelites walking through the dry riverbed.

# 2. Monumental Love

*Kids will use paper egg cartons to form a unique monument to God's love.*

**Theme:** God wants us to remember his goodness and faithfulness.

**Scripture Spotlight 1:** "They carried with them the twelve rocks taken from the Jordan..." "What do these rocks mean?" Tell them, "Israel crossed the Jordan River on dry land"'" (Joshua 4:20-22).

**Scripture Spotlight 2:** "Your promises are proven, so I, your servant, love them" (Psalm 119:140).

**Collect:** Paper egg cartons (made from recycled paper), scissors, yarn, a plastic yarn needle, and markers.

# Here's What to Do:

Before class, cut the lids off the paper egg cartons. You may want to save the lids for other crafts.

Give each child the bottom of a paper egg carton and a 2-foot length of yarn. (If you have more than 15 students, you may want to give each child one-half of an egg carton.) Explain that kids will be working together to build a monument similar to the one the Israelites built when they crossed the Jordan River.

Set out markers and give kids a few minutes to personalize the bumpy sides of the cartons by writing their names on them and drawing pictures of things they enjoy and of things that show God's love. When kids are finished decorating, call two volunteers forward and have them hold their cartons together vertically with the long inside edges together. Then show kids how to use the yarn and the plastic yarn needle to sew one edge of the cartons together. Have students tie a knot at the end of the yarn to secure it. Explain that each student will sew one edge of his or her carton to the one on the end. Be sure kids sew the cartons so the rounded egg holders are on the outside.

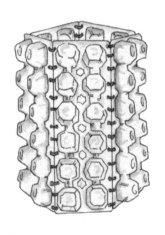

Kids who haven't finished can continue to decorate their cartons while they wait for their turn. Help the last student sew his or her carton to the open edge of the first carton to form a cylinder. Invite students to walk around and enjoy what others drew on the monument they've made to God's love.

# For Further Fun:

● Have kids fill the cylinder with canned goods, toys, clothes, or new blankets to donate to a homeless shelter.

● Instead of having kids work with intact cartons, have them cut the egg cups apart then stack them together to make a unique "rock."

# 3. And They All Came Tumbling Down

*Kids will form an assembly line to make clay bricks and build the wall of Jericho.*

**Theme:** God accomplishes his purposes.

**Scripture Spotlight 1:** "When the priests blew the trumpets, the people shouted. At the sound of the trumpets and the people's shout, the walls fell, and everyone ran straight into the city. So the Israelites defeated that city" (Joshua 6:20).

**Scripture Spotlight 2:** "We know that in everything God works for the good of those who love him. They are the people he called, because that was his plan" (Romans 8:28).

**Collect:** Cookie sheets; a kitchen oven; for each group of four or five kids: 4 cups of flour, 1 cup of salt, 1½ to 1¾ cups of warm water, a large bowl, and a mixing spoon (optional: toy kazoos)

## Here's What to Do:

If possible, do this craft during a longer craft time so that bricks can be baked, *or* make this a two-week project and allow the bricks to air-dry.

Form brick-making groups of four or five children. Have group members designate three people to be the brick mixers and one to be the brick baker.

Have two of the brick mixers mix the clay ingredients (4 cups of flour, 1 cup of salt, and 1½ to 1¾ cups of warm water) together. Then instruct the other brick mixer to knead the dough for several minutes. When the dough is mixed sufficiently, have all group members mold it into small rectangular bricks approximately 2×3 inches and no more than ¾ inch thick (thinner bricks dry faster). Then instruct the brick baker to assemble the bricks on a cookie sheet. With adult supervision, the children should bake the bricks at 300 degrees for about 30 minutes. If you do not have access to a kitchen oven, let the bricks air-dry until your next class time.

When the bricks have baked and cooled, show kids how to work together to create a wall with their bricks. Then distribute toy kazoos and have the class simulate the fall of Jericho by counting to seven and blowing the kazoos to make the walls fall. (Everyone gently knocks the wall over together.) Children can take turns being Joshua and giving the signal to knock down the wall.

## For Further Fun:

● Create bricks by covering tissue boxes or cereal boxes with brown paper sacks cut into pieces. Kids can create a "bricked" look on the brown paper by doing wall rubbings before they wrap the boxes.

# 4. When Time Stood Still

*Kids will make their own colorful sun visors.*

## Theme: Our God is an awesome God.

## Scripture Spotlight 1: "On the day that the Lord gave up the Amorites to the Israelites, Joshua stood before all the people of Israel and said to the Lord: 'Sun, stand still over Gibeon. Moon, stand still over the Valley of Aijalon.' So the sun stood still, and the moon stopped until the people defeated their enemies" (Joshua 10:12-13).

## Scripture Spotlight 2: "So, as the Scripture says, 'If someone wants to brag, he should brag only about the Lord' " (1 Corinthians 1:31).

## Collect: Newspapers, plastic sun visors, puffy paint in assorted colors, sequins, glue, and colored glue

## Here's What to Do:

Spread newspapers on a table, then set out puffy paint, sequins, and glues. Remind children that God caused the sun to stand still in the sky until Joshua's army had defeated its enemies. Have them imagine an afternoon that lasted a whole day! Explain that kids will make sun visors to keep the afternoon sun out of their eyes. Distribute plastic sun visors to students and allow them to decorate their visors anyway they wish. Encourage kids to be creative and make visors that are truly unique!

## For Further Fun:

● Allow kids to use the puffy paints to decorate inexpensive sunglasses to match their visors.

● Have a sun-visor parade. Kids can model their visors for adults or other classes and retell the story of the defeat of the Amorites.

# 5. A Household of Strength

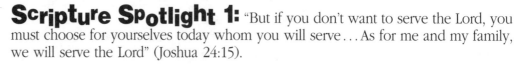

*Kids will use stenciled bricks to make great doorstops.*

**Theme:** God wants our families to follow him.

**Scripture Spotlight 1:** "But if you don't want to serve the Lord, you must choose for yourselves today whom you will serve...As for me and my family, we will serve the Lord" (Joshua 24:15).

**Scripture Spotlight 2:** "Everyone who hears my words and obeys them is like a wise man who built his house on a rock" (Matthew 7:24).

**Collect:** Bricks, acrylic paints, paintbrushes, photocopies of the "Household of Strength" stencil (p. 25), pencils, scissors, colored felt, and glue

## Here's What to Do:

Before class, cut out the "Household of Strength" stencils (p. 25).

Give each student a brick, a handout, and access to the acrylic paints and paintbrushes. Explain that kids will be making doorstops for their homes.

Have kids use the stencils and paints to decorate the bricks. Older students may want to write, "As for me and my family, we will serve the Lord" (Joshua 24:15b) on their bricks or decorate them freehand. Then help kids trace around their bricks onto pieces of colored felt. Kids can cut out the felt and glue it to the bottom of their bricks for padding.

## For Further Fun:

● Kids can add their names and the names of their family members to the doorstops.

● Take kids outside and have them each find a large rock to decorate as a doorstop for another door in the house.

# Household Of Strength

# Gideon

**"I**f God loves me, why can't I win this game? or get along with my sister? or have peace on earth?" These are the kinds of questions that occur to kids. Gideon had similar questions for the angel of the Lord: "If the Lord is with us, why are we having so much trouble?" (Judges 6:13). Gideon was about to embark on an adventure that would prove to him that God provides in even seemingly impossible situations. Use the activities in this section to help children learn that they can depend on God to give them everything they'll need to do his work!*

**1.** The angel of the Lord came to speak to Gideon while he was threshing wheat in a wine press. The angel brought an extraordinary message: God wanted Gideon to lead the Israelites to victory (Judges 6:14). Use Idea 1, "An Angel Messenger," to help kids remember that God calls them to do his work.

**2.** God called Gideon to save Israel from its enemies, the Midianites. The first step was to announce to them that the territory belonged to God, not to Baal and other idols. Gideon did this by tearing down the idols of the Midianites and constructing an altar to the Lord. Use Idea 2, "A Pure Altar," to show children that God protects them as they do his work.

**3.** When it was time to battle the Midianites, God gave Gideon an unusual strategy. God had instructed Gideon to send the majority of his army home, retaining only 300 men to fight combined armies of over 100,000 soldiers. It was the custom of the time to have only a few trumpeters to call the men to battle. Instead, Gideon gave each of his men a trumpet. When the Midianites heard the racket, they panicked, assuming they were outnumbered! Use Idea 3, "Tubular Trumpets," to help kids realize that when they work together, they can accomplish God's plans.

**4.** Gideon equipped his soldiers with more than trumpets. He also gave each one a reminder of God's presence—a light. Kids will remember that God is with them as they make Idea 4, "Luminous Lights."

# 1. An Angel Messenger

*Kids will construct message holders to remind them of God's Word.*

**Theme:** The Lord calls us to do his work.

**Scripture Spotlight 1:** "I am the one who is sending you" (Judges 6:14).

**Scripture Spotlight 2:** "You can trust the One who calls you" (1 Thessalonians 5:24a).

**Collect:** Bibles, unlined 3×5 cards, plastic spoons, 5-inch lengths of white or silver crinkled paper ribbon or 1-inch craft ribbon, yellow yarn, glue, permanent markers, and scissors

## Here's What to Do:

Set out unlined 3×5 cards, plastic spoons, 5-inch lengths of white or silver crinkled paper ribbon, yellow yarn, glue, scissors, and permanent markers. Explain that kids will be making a messenger angel like the one who brought an important message to Gideon. Give each student a 3×5 card and have him or her write a favorite verse on it. Then instruct students to hold the index cards horizontally and glue a spoon to the back of each card so the rounded side of the spoon faces the front (see diagram). While the glue is drying, give two lengths of ribbon to each child. Help kids glue one end of each ribbon to the spoon handle then wrap the other ends around to the sides of the cards. Have students use the permanent markers and yarn to decorate the "faces" of the spoons to look like angels' faces. Then show kids how to gather the ends of the ribbons and glue them to the cards as shown in the margin.

## For Further Fun:

● Use this same method, but instead of index cards, have children use squares of cork board (available at most craft and variety stores). They can pin messages to each other's boards.

● Give kids pads of self-adhesive notes to glue to their index cards. Then provide craft magnets for kids to glue to the back of their messenger angels.

# 2. A Pure Altar

*Kids will construct an altar using soap "stones."*

**Theme:** God protects us from our enemies.

**Scripture Spotlight 1:** "The men of the city asked each other, 'Who did this?' After they asked many questions, someone told them, 'Gideon son of Joash did this.' So they said to Joash, 'Bring your son out... He must die!' " (Judges 6:29-30).

**Scripture Spotlight 2:** "The Lord loves justice and will not leave those who worship him. He will always protect them" (Psalm 37:28a).

**Collect:** Soap flakes (Ivory Snow works best), bowls, water, teaspoons, measuring cups, and paper towels

## Here's What to Do:

Give each child a bowl and have each one mix 2 cups of soap flakes with 2 teaspoons of water. Allow kids a few moments to mix and squeeze the mixture into a soap clay. Tell children that they'll have a chance to work together to build a pure altar to God as Gideon did after he tore down the false idols.

Have kids mold their soap clay into small stones approximately the size of their palms. Remind them to make the top and bottom of the stones slightly flat so they

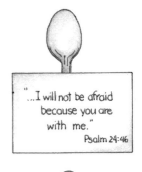

can be stacked on top of each other. As kids finish their altar blocks, have them bring them to the center of the table and begin stacking their blocks with others' to build an altar. Students can fill in the gaps with a paste made from soap flakes mixed with a little water. Let the altar dry thoroughly.

## For Further Fun:

● Have kids draw on 3×5 cards pictures of how God has protected them. Have them thank the Lord for his protection as they leave their cards on the soap altar.

● When the altar has dried, allow each person to chip off a piece of it and thank God for his righteousness and protection.

# 3. Tubular Trumpets

*Kids will make musical instruments from plumbing supplies.*

**Theme:** God gives us equally important jobs.

**Scripture Spotlight 1:** "Gideon divided the three hundred men into three groups. He gave each man a trumpet... When Gideon's three hundred men blew their trumpets, the Lord made all the Midianites fight each other with their swords!" (Judges 7:16a, 22a).

**Scripture Spotlight 2:** "Each part does its own work to make the whole body grow and be strong with love" (Ephesians 4:16b).

**Collect:** One-inch PVC pipe, 1½-inch PVC pipe, duct tape, sandpaper, ribbon scraps, permanent markers, streamers, buttons, and craft glue

## Here's What to Do:

duct tape

Before purchasing the PVC pipe, make sure that the small pipe slides into the larger one. Then, before class, saw the PVC pipe into 1-foot sections. (Use a power saw or ask your hardware store to do this for you.)

Form pairs and have each partner choose the role of either a taper or a sander. Give each taper two pieces of the 1-inch PVC pipe and each sander two pieces of the 1½-inch PVC pipe. Have each taper put a strip of duct tape at the top end of his or her sections of pipe so that the tape completely covers the holes. Have each sander sand the top edges of his or her pipes until they're smooth. Then have children slide the bottom of the smaller tubes through the top of the larger tubes and push them until the smaller tubes extend about ½ inch beyond the larger ones. Show them how to put the top of the large tubes up to their mouths and, holding their lips tightly together, blow into the mouthpieces. As they pull the smaller tubes down, the tone will deepen. It takes some practice! Tell children that when Gideon's army blew their trumpets, they frightened the other, larger armies away.

The outside of the trumpets may then be decorated with ribbon scraps, streamers, buttons, or permanent markers.

## For Further Fun:

● Have kids try to match their trumpets' tones. The sound depends on the shape of their lips and the extension of the inner tubes of the trumpets. Using a piano or other instrument, try to find certain notes with the trumpets. Have kids mark the notes on the sides of the inner tubes.

● Construct other tubular trumpets, varying the sizes of the PVC pipes. The narrower the pipe, the higher the tone and the more difficult it is to produce a clear sound.

# 4. Luminous Lights

*Kids will work in pairs to create bags of light.*

**Theme:** God gives us reminders of his presence.

**Scripture Spotlight 1:** "He gave each man...an empty jar with a burning torch inside" (Judges 7:16).

**Scripture Spotlight 2:** "The Lord is my light and the one who saves me. I fear no one" (Psalm 27:1a).

**Collect:** Paper lunch bags, scissors, pencils, towels, straight pins, photocopies of the "Luminous Lights" handout (p. 30), and flashlights

## Here's What to Do:

Before class, make enough photocopies of the "Luminous Lights" handout (p. 30) for every two children to have one.

Have children form pairs and have each partner choose to be either an artist or a designer. Give each pair a "Luminous Lights" handout and instruct one partner to cut out one of the stencils. Then have the artist trace it onto both sides of the paper lunch bag. Have the designer lay the bag on a folded towel and carefully poke a straight pin along the lines so the pinholes are evenly spaced. Have each pair repeat the process on the opposite side of the bag. When each pair has made one bag, explain that Gideon's soldiers went into battle with torches that were covered with jars. Tell them that the light might have shone through cracks in the jars or from the bottom of the jars. Have kids place flashlights in the bottom of the bags and watch the light shine through the designs. Partners may each trace a design and switch roles to make additional bags.

## For Further Fun:

● Explain that kids can take the bags home and fill them with about 1 inch of sand. Under adult supervision, they can put a small, lighted votive candle inside each bag and display the luminaria outside or in a window.

● Children may make their own designs or write their names with the straight pins.

# Luminous Lights

# Elijah

**E**lijah preached forcefully against idol worship. As a result, he spent much of his lifetime hiding from King Ahab and Queen Jezebel, who would have killed him on sight. But God protected Elijah by sending ravens to feed him during a drought that lasted three years. When Elijah challenged 450 prophets of Baal to a showdown between Baal and God, God honored Elijah's prayer and set the altar ablaze. At the end of Elijah's life, God took Elijah to heaven in a whirlwind, making him one of only two people taken to heaven without dying. This powerful prophet struggled with fear, loneliness, and discouragement, yet bravely carried out God's commands.

**1.** During a long drought, God provided for Elijah's every need. He sent Elijah to live by a stream that provided water, then sent birds to feed him (1 Kings 17:6). Kids can express their gratitude for God's provision in Idea 1, "Birds of a Feather."

**2.** Elijah challenged 450 prophets of Baal to a contest to show them that God is the only true and powerful God and that Baal was nothing but a lifeless idol. The prophets tried for hours to get Baal to hear them and answer their prayers, but to no avail. Then after Elijah prayed a short and simple prayer, God sent fire from heaven that consumed Elijah's sacrifice, the altar, and the ground around it (1 Kings 18:22-38). Use Idea 2, "Fire From Heaven," to help children learn that God answers prayer in mighty ways.

**3.** God told Elijah to declare that there would be no rain. Elijah obeyed, and there was no rain for three years. But after the victory over 450 prophets of Baal, Elijah announced that a heavy rain was on its way. Soon dark clouds covered the sky, the wind began to blow, and a heavy rain started to fall. God had shown his power in a way that would be hard to forget! Use Idea 3, "Dark Clouds," to help children see that God is powerful.

**4.** Even after God's mighty display of power, Elijah ran and hid in a cave when Queen Jezebel threatened to kill him. God told Elijah, "Go, stand in front of me on the mountain, and I will pass by you" (1 Kings 19:11a). There was an earthquake, a windstorm, and a fire, but God wasn't in those frightening events. When Elijah heard a soft, quiet sound, he went out to meet with God. Use Idea 4, "Gentle Sounds," to help children see that God gently cares for his children.

**5.** Everything that happened to Elijah was dramatic. What could be a more fitting end to Elijah's life on earth than to be taken to heaven in a whirlwind (2 Kings 2:11)? God rewarded Elijah by taking him to heaven before he died. Use Idea 5, "Chariots of Cheese," to talk about heaven with the children in your class.

# 1. Birds of a Feather

*Kids will make feather paintings of things they're thankful for.*

**Theme:** God provides for us in unique ways.

**Scripture Spotlight 1:** "The birds brought Elijah bread and meat every morning and evening" (1 Kings 17:6a).

**Scripture Spotlight 2:** "How great is your goodness that you have stored up for those who fear you, that you have given to those who trust you" (Psalm 31:19).

**Collect:** Coated paper, newspapers, tempera paints (primary colors work well), feathers (available at most craft stores), and pie tins

## Here's What to Do:

Form foursomes. Have each group form a circle in one area of the room. Tell students that they'll be painting with feathers as reminders of the birds that God sent to provide for Elijah. Instruct groups to cover their work spaces with newspapers. Give each group three pie tins with a different color of tempera paint in each. Then give each group a stack of coated paper and a handful of feathers.

Encourage kids to use the feathers to paint pictures of things that God has provided for them, such as food, homes, trees, family members, or animals. If kids need to mix colors, have them do so on their picture. This not only creates a blended, marbled effect, but also prevents paints from becoming muddy.

Allow students to experiment with their feather brushes and draw several pictures. Post the pictures around your room as reminders of God's goodness and provision.

## For Further Fun:

● Play a cassette of bubbling-stream and bird noises while kids work, reminding them that God sent birds to provide for Elijah.

● Kids can work together on a mural, using feather dusters as paintbrushes. This is a good medium for drawing a jungle or nature scene.

# 2. Fire From Heaven

*Kids will make pictures about Elijah and the prophets of Baal.*

**Theme:** God's works are amazing!

**Scripture Spotlight 1:** "Then fire from the Lord came down and burned the sacrifice, the wood, the stones, and the ground around the altar. It also dried up the water in the ditch" (1 Kings 18:38).

**Scripture Spotlight 2:** "Say to God, 'Your works are amazing! Because your power is great, your enemies fall before you' " (Psalm 66:3).

**Collect:** Wax paper; gray and brown construction paper; scissors; an iron; newspaper; a towel; water; a cheese grater; and red, orange, and yellow crayons

## Here's What to Do:

Have children cut out stones and wood from gray and brown construction paper and create altars on sheets of wax paper. They also may cut out figures to represent Elijah.

Instruct kids to grate the crayons, being careful not to scrape their fingers and knuckles. Have them scatter the shavings on top of the altars to represent the fire. Then have them cover their pictures with other sheets of wax paper and carefully bring their pictures to you.

Set up an iron on a table near an electrical outlet so children won't trip over the cord. Place a stack of newspaper on the table. Have students take turns putting their pictures on top of the newspaper then sprinkling water on the top layer of wax paper. Cover each picture with a towel and iron it with a hot iron so the dribbled water turns to steam. When you lift the towel, the altar will be aglow with flames of "fire."

## For Further Fun:

● Dribble more water on the towel and put the hot iron on it. Have the children listen to the sputter and watch the steam rise. Talk about other things that show God's power. Thank God together for being a powerful God.

# 3. Dark Clouds

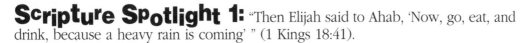

*Kids will work together to make a huge cloud to hang in the middle of the classroom.*

**Theme:** God is powerful.

**Scripture Spotlight 1:** "Then Elijah said to Ahab, 'Now, go, eat, and drink, because a heavy rain is coming' " (1 Kings 18:41).

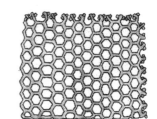

**Scripture Spotlight 2:** "Who has the wisdom to count the clouds? Who can pour water from the jars of the sky when the dust becomes hard and the clumps of dirt stick together?" (Job 38:37-38).

**Collect:** Chicken wire, wire clippers, pliers, masking tape, newspaper, chairs, work gloves, facial tissue, blue construction paper, tape, scissors, and monofilament fishing line

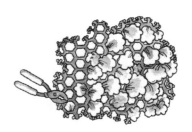

## Here's What to Do:

Have older children help you make a large three-dimensional cloud shape out of chicken wire. Use wire clippers to cut an 8- to 10-foot-long section of chicken wire. You may want to wear work gloves to protect your hands from the wire ends. Fold both ends of the wire into the middle and fasten them together by bending and wrapping the cut, straight wires from one end over the loops of the other end. *Cover all wire ends with masking tape.* Have kids stuff the middle with balls of newspaper.

Use pliers to push and pull on the chicken wire so it looks like a bumpy cloud. Prop the cloud shape on chairs and show children how to crumple and tuck facial tissue into all of the holes of the chicken wire. Be sure the edges of the tissues stick out so the cloud looks puffy.

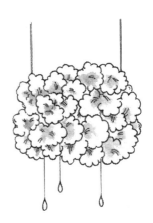

Cut two lengths of the monofilament fishing line. Have older kids help you attach the fishing line to opposite ends of the top of the cloud shape and hang the cloud from the ceiling.

Have the children cut large raindrops from blue construction paper. Help them tape their raindrops to different lengths of fishing line then tape the line to the underside of the cloud.

## For Further Fun:

● Have children draw pictures on the raindrops of the good things that come from God. Have each child walk under the rain cloud and imagine that God is showering him or her with good gifts.

● Gather under the cloud and create a storm. Have kids begin by rubbing their hands together for 30 seconds, snapping their fingers for 30 seconds, then slapping their legs for 30 seconds. Encourage them to get louder and louder, gradually building the storm. Kids can taper off the storm by reversing their actions—snapping their fingers for 30 seconds then rubbing their hands together for 30 seconds.

# 4. Gentle Sounds

*Kids will make aeolian harps to remind them of God's quiet presence.*

**Theme:** God is gentle with his children.

**Scripture Spotlight 1:** "After the fire, there was a quiet, gentle sound. When Elijah heard it, he covered his face with his coat and went out and stood at the entrance to the cave" (1 Kings 19:12b-13).

**Scripture Spotlight 2:** "God says, 'Be quiet and know that I am God' " (Psalm 46:10a).

**Collect:** 2×4-inch pieces of lumber cut into 2-foot lengths, clean cloths, nails, eye screws, hammers, craft sticks, monofilament or thin wire, medium-weight sandpaper, acrylic paint, paintbrushes, white glue, pencils, rulers, and a hot-glue gun

## Here's What to Do:

Give each child four craft sticks. Have kids glue two sticks together so the broad, flat sides touch. Instruct them to glue their other two sticks together in the same way. Set these aside to dry.

Give each child a 2-foot length of a 2×4-inch piece of lumber and a piece of medium-weight sandpaper. Have kids sand all surfaces of the boards until they're smooth then wipe the sawdust off the boards with clean cloths. Set out acrylic paint and paintbrushes and allow children to paint the top and sides of their boards.

While the paint is drying, have the children measure the glued-together sticks. Have them use pencils to mark on both sets of sticks the center point and points 1½ inches on either side of the center point. Help children use a glue gun to glue the thin side of the sticks to the painted boards. The sticks should be positioned two inches in from the ends of the boards and should be parallel to the ends of the boards.

After the glue has dried, help each child pound three nails near one end of the board, parallel with the pencil marks. Then help children screw the eye screws in at the opposite end of the boards. The eye screws should also line up with the pencil marks. Help each child attach three lengths of monofilament or thin wire between the nails and the eye screws. The wire *must* be stretched tightly. Turn the eye screws to further tighten the wires.

Have students put these aeolian harps in their windows at their homes. If they open the windows just a little when there's a breeze, the air will make the strings vibrate with gentle sounds.

## For Further Fun:

● Have everyone blow across the strings and try to get them to make sounds. Talk about the things that are easy for God to do but that are hard for us to do.

● Have the class *gently* strum their strings as they sing a quiet praise song such as "God Is So Good."

# 5. Chariots of Cheese

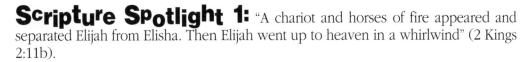

*Kids will enjoy tasty chariots of cheese.*

**Theme:** God takes his followers to heaven.

**Scripture Spotlight 1:** "A chariot and horses of fire appeared and separated Elijah from Elisha. Then Elijah went up to heaven in a whirlwind" (2 Kings 2:11b).

**Scripture Spotlight 2:** "There are many rooms in my Father's house; I would not tell you this if it were not true. I am going there to prepare a place for you" (John 14:2).

**Collect:** Refrigerator biscuit dough, grated cheddar cheese, baking sheets, rolling pins or large cups, and wax paper

## Here's What to Do:

Have kids wash their hands. Give each student three pieces of refrigerator biscuit dough and a sheet of wax paper. Set the grated cheddar cheese and rolling pins or large cups in the middle of the table so everyone can reach them.

Using a cup or a rolling pin, show kids how to roll one biscuit into a small rectangle. Then have students press their other biscuits into the bottom of the rectangles to make wheels.

Allow kids to sprinkle their chariots with grated cheese to resemble fire before transferring the chariots to the baking sheets. Bake according to package directions.

## For Further Fun:

● As children enjoy their snack, have them talk about things they're anticipating about heaven.

# Daniel and His Friends

**I**f there had been a who's who in the kingdom of Babylon, Daniel and his friends certainly would have been included. They were truly outstanding young men—studious, handsome, and dedicated to God (Daniel 1:4-6). Their faithfulness to God and God's faithfulness to them proved to be the only things they could depend on no matter what happened. Your kids can depend on God's presence, too. Use the activities in this section to help kids learn that God is always there for them, too.

**1.** Daniel and his friends were handpicked to serve in the palace of King Nebuchadnezzar. They had to be quick learners so they could function in their new country. God was with them as they learned a new language and culture (Daniel 1:17). Use Idea 1, "Cuneiform Blocks," to help kids experience the difficulty of Daniel's schooling.

**2.** Nebuchadnezzar rewarded the wisdom of Daniel and his friends, but he wasn't ready to adopt the ways of their God. He set up a statue that he ordered everyone to worship (Daniel 3:1-6). With Idea 2, "Sugar Dudes," help kids remember how useless it is to worship anything other than the one true God.

**3.** Shadrach, Meshach, and Abednego had the opportunity to experience the presence of God firsthand when they were thrown into the fiery furnace (Daniel 3:21). Use Idea 3, "Fan the Flames," to help kids recognize that God will be with them always.

**4.** Darius the Mede had to learn about God's presence in a different way. Though he was fond of Daniel, his advisors convinced him to make a law that would force him to condemn Daniel to death. Use Idea 4, "Sweet Seals," to help kids remember that God walks with them even when their most loyal friends desert them.

**5.** Strengthened by a lifetime of trusting in God, Daniel spent the night in a den full of ferocious lions. He walked away from certain death, giving praise to God for sending an angel to save him. Idea 5, "Hear Me Roar," will show kids that God can protect them from even the most frightening circumstances.

# 1. Cuneiform Blocks

*Kids will block print with cuneiform designs.*

**Theme:** God is with us as we learn new things.

**Scripture Spotlight 1:** "God gave these four young men wisdom and the ability to learn many things…" (Daniel 1:17).

**Scripture Spotlight 2:** "Teach the wise, and they will become even wiser; teach good people, and they will learn even more" (Proverbs 9:9).

**Collect:** Wood blocks, thick twine or cord, tissue paper, copies of the "New Way of Talkin' " handout (p. 38) enlarged or reduced to fit your blocks, pencils, permanent markers, glue, newspaper, tempera paint, and construction paper

## Here's What to Do:

Before class, make enough photocopies of the "New Way of Talkin' " handout (p. 38) for every four students to have one.

Form groups of four. Give each person in the group a number between one and four and explain that each group will form its own assembly line.

All the ones will use pencils to trace the patterns from the handouts onto tissue paper. Then the twos will place the tissue paper on the wood blocks, choose cuneiform patterns they like, and draw over them with permanent markers. The markers will seep through the tissue and mark the wood with the patterns. The threes will take the blocks and outline the cuneiform patterns with glue, then the fours will place the thick twine or cord on the glue. Allow the glue to dry completely.

While the glue is drying, explain the meaning of each cuneiform character on the handout. When the glue is dry, have a volunteer from each group pour some tempera paint onto the newspapers then blot the papers together to distribute the paint. Show kids how to use the paint pads like stamp pads and press the cuneiform blocks into them. Let kids take turns stamping their characters on construction paper.

## For Further Fun:

● Have the kids print messages with the blocks. Then let others try to decipher their meanings.

● Put together several cuneiform designs to make a class motto or slogan. Print these characters on a T-shirt with fabric paint or on stationery with an ink pad.

# 2. Sugar Dudes

*Trios will use "gold blocks" to build statues.*

**Theme:** There is only one God, and he is strong—other gods are fakes.

**Scripture Spotlight 1:** "We want you, O king, to know this: We will not serve your gods or worship the gold statue you have set up" (Daniel 3:18b).

**Scripture Spotlight 2:** "God has said this, and I have heard it over and over: God is strong" (Psalm 62:11).

**Collect:** Sugar cubes, gold spray paint, glue, a cookie sheet for each group, and pitchers of water

# New Way of Talkin'

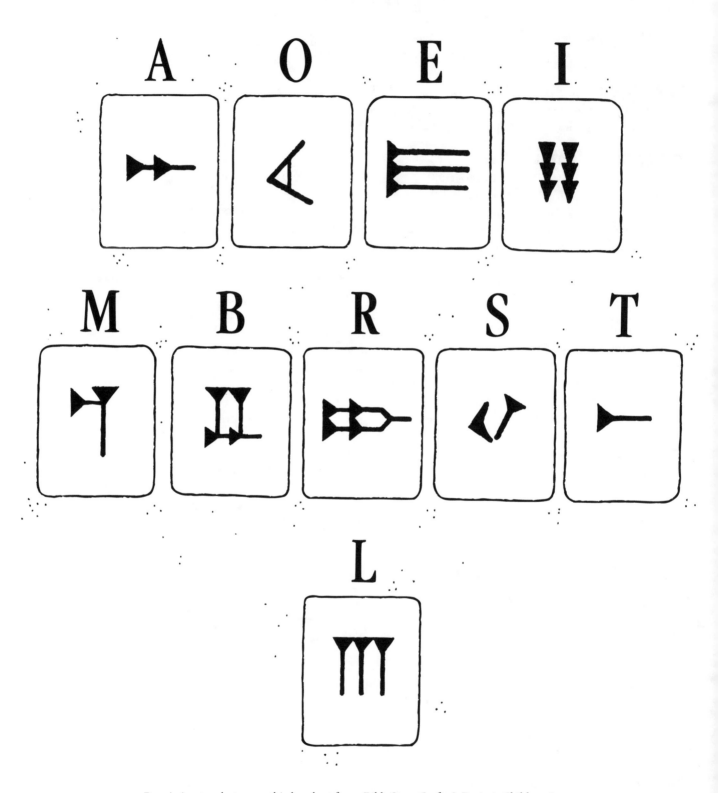

## Here's What to Do:

Before class, *lightly* spray the sugar cubes with gold spray paint, being careful to hold the can far away from the cubes to prevent saturation. Form trios, who will use the gold blocks to construct statues on the cookie sheets. Explain that King Nebuchadnezzar built himself an enormous gold statue.

When all the statues are completed, talk about God's strength. Ask children how strong they think their statues are. Have them imagine that the water in the pitchers represents problems or challenges, then begin to pour water on the statue for each problem children can think of. Watch the statues crumble as they're saturated with water. Remind kids that only God is strong and will stay with them through all their problems and challenges.

## For Further Fun:

● Have kids use their remaining gold cubes to make frames for this Scripture verse: "God has said this, and I have heard it over and over: God is strong" (Psalm 62:11). Attach paper clips to the back for hangers.

● Allow kids to suck on unpainted sugar cubes and tell about sweet things they love about God.

# 3. Fan the Flames

*Kids will cool themselves with fans of fire!*

## Theme: God is with us in dangerous situations.

## Scripture Spotlight 1: "The king said, 'Look! I see four men walking around in the fire. They are not tied up, and they are not burned. The fourth man looks like a son of the gods...No other god can save his people like this' " (Daniel 3:25, 29).

## Scripture Spotlight 2: "You are my hiding place. You protect me from my troubles" (Psalm 32:7a).

## Collect: Yellow cellophane, red cellophane, glue sticks, scissors, craft sticks, and paper plates

## Here's What to Do:

Set out the paper plates, yellow and red cellophane, scissors, and glue sticks. Tell children that they'll be making paper fans that look like flames to remind them of the fiery furnace that couldn't burn Shadrach, Meshach, and Abednego.

Distribute paper plates and craft sticks, then allow children to decorate the plates by gluing different shapes of the colored cellophane to both sides. Encourage children to cut out flame shapes and make the cellophane extend past the edges of the plates. Then have kids glue craft sticks to the plates as handles. When the glue has dried, show children how to fan themselves with the paper plates. Your cool classroom will be full of fiery flames!

## For Further Fun:

● Act out the story of Shadrach, Meshach, and Abednego from Daniel 3:13-28. Have children fan the actors with their fiery fans to make a surprisingly cool furnace.

● Have kids use their fans for a game of Hot and Cold Tag. When children are tagged by the "Heatmeister," they must stand and "burn" by waving their fiery fans until "Chilly Willy" tags and frees them.

# 4. Sweet Seals

*Kids will make candy treats with stamps and chocolate.*

**Theme:** God is with us when everyone turns away.

**Scripture Spotlight 1:** "So King Darius gave the order, and Daniel was brought in and thrown into the lion's den. The king said to Daniel, 'May the God you serve all the time save you!...' The king used his signet ring and the rings of his royal officers to put special seals on the rock. This ensured that no one would move the rock and bring Daniel out. Then King Darius went back to his palace" (Daniel 6:16-18b).

**Scripture Spotlight 2:** "I have one who speaks for me in heaven; the one who is on my side is high above. The one who speaks for me is my friend" (Job 16:19-20).

**Collect:** Melted chocolate chips, clean rubber stamps, wax paper, and a spoon or a frosting bag

## Here's What to Do:

Form pairs and give each pair a sheet of wax paper. Have kids fold up the bottom third of their papers then fold the top third down. Drop 2 tablespoons of melted chocolate chips onto the wax paper to seal the folded edge. Warn kids that the chocolate may still be warm so they shouldn't touch it. Have kids watch for the chocolate to begin to lose its glossiness. Then it will be ready for imprinting. Show kids how to gently push the clean rubber stamps into the soft chocolate. Explain that this is similar to what King Darius did with the wax that sealed Daniel in the lion's den.

Have kids wait for their chocolate seals to cool and harden, then allow them to peel the chocolate off the papers. Instruct kids to trade treats with another pair to remind each other that God gives his sweet love to us freely.

### For Further Fun:

● Have kids make more chocolate seals to give away. Wrap each in a piece of colored cellophane.

● Try using different flavors of baking chips.

● Allow kids to unbend clean paper clips and use the points of them to imprint their own initials in the chocolate.

# 5. Hear Me Roar

*Kids will create colorful lion masks.*

**Theme:** God is with us when we're scared.

**Scripture Spotlight 1:** "My God sent his angel to close the lions' mouths. They have not hurt me" (Daniel 6:22a).

**Scripture Spotlight 2:** "Even if I walk through a very dark valley, I will not be afraid, because you are with me" (Psalm 23:4a).

**Collect:** 12-inch plastic saucers (usually placed under houseplants to catch excess water), 12-inch lengths of string, yellow and brown yarn, pencils, yellow felt, scissors, a stapler, and glue

# Here's What to Do:

Give each child a 12-inch plastic saucer and a pair of scissors. Set all other materials in the middle of the table so everyone can reach them. Instruct kids to cut out the middle of their saucers, leaving plastic rings for them to work with. The rings should be a little larger than the kids' faces. (Collect the flat middle pieces for use in other crafts.)

Have kids hold the plastic rings up to their faces and make pencil dots where the rings meet their ears. Then allow kids to use scissors to poke small holes where they've marked the dots. Have kids thread a 12-inch length of string through each hole and tie knots to keep the strings from slipping through the holes. Kids will tie the strings together to hold the masks in place.

Show kids how to cut two lion ears apiece from yellow felt. Kids may choose to cut simple triangles (approximately 3 inches tall) or to create a more rounded look. Help kids staple the ears to the top of the plastic rings. The ears may fold down or stand up.

Next, have kids cut lengths of yellow and brown yarn between 5 and 7 inches long, dip one end of each piece of the yarn in glue, then pinch both ends together to make loops. Kids can then glue the cut ends of the loops to the outside edge of the plastic rings. Allow kids to continue adding loops until they think their "manes" are full enough.

When the glue has dried, help children tie on their masks.

# For Further Fun:

● Have kids draw lion faces on each other using face paint or watercolor paints.

● Kids can act out the story of Daniel in the den of lions by growling fiercely during the story until you mention the angel who shut the lions' mouths.

# David

**D**avid's life shows us God's ability to use ordinary people to achieve monumental tasks. Just imagine a young shepherd boy rising to power as a conqueror and king. Though kids today may feel too small and unimportant to do anything significant for God, the Bible clearly shows that God can use anyone to accomplish his plans. Use the ideas in this section to help kids realize that God can use them just as he used David.

**1.** David spent many hours with his father's sheep, watching over them, guiding them to safe grazing areas, and protecting them from predators. Using only his bare hands and a sling, David killed a lion and a bear (1 Samuel 17:34-37). This same sling helped him kill the giant Goliath as well. Use Idea 1, "Sure Shot," to help kids visualize the simple tool that David used to conquer a mighty giant.

**2.** The book of Psalms shows us that David was also a skillful musician. In fact, 1 Samuel 18:10-11 tells us that David played the harp regularly. Use Idea 2, "Joyful Noisemakers," to help kids make their own instruments to play.

**3.** David and Jonathan, Saul's son, were best friends. Although Saul hated David, Jonathan loved him like a brother and protected him from Saul. When David fled into the hills, Jonathan gave his armor, sword, bow, and belt to David as gifts of friendship. Idea 3, "Between You and Me," will give kids a chance to make special gifts for their special friends.

**4.** Even after Jonathan died, David remembered their friendship by taking care of Jonathan's son, Mephibosheth. He honored Mephibosheth by asking him to dine at the king's table each day. Idea 4, "Serving up a Smile," will allow kids to create their own tables they can use to serve others.

**5.** David was a great warrior, and God always watched over him in battle. Use Idea 5, "A Shield Around Me," to help kids make their own shields for protection.

# 1. Sure Shot

*Kids will create slingshots for fun.*

**Theme:** God protected David.

**Scripture Spotlight 1:** "He took a stone from his bag, put it into his sling, and slung it. The stone hit the Philistine and went deep into his forehead, and Goliath fell facedown on the ground" (1 Samuel 17:49).

**Scripture Spotlight 2:** "The Lord is my strength and shield. I trust him, and he helps me" (Psalm 28:7a).

**Collect:** 1 yard of leather lacing for each child, one 4×2-inch square of leather or vinyl per child, nails, hammers, blocks of wood, markers, rulers, scissors, and used paper or newspaper

# Here's What to Do:

Give each child a 4×2-inch square of leather or vinyl and 1 yard of leather lacing. Form pairs and give each pair a marker, a ruler, scissors, a hammer, a nail, and a block of wood.

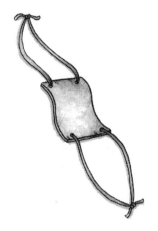

Have partners cut their leather lacing into two equal pieces then work together to measure and mark their leather rectangles ½ inch from each corner. Show kids how to lay rectangles over wood blocks and pound nails to make a hole at each of the marked corners. When kids have made four holes in their rectangles, have them thread one piece of leather lacing into two of the holes and the other piece into the other two. Show students how to tie the ends of the laces together.

Have kids crumple up pieces of used paper or newspaper and practice using their slingshots. They'll need to hold the leather lacing and swing the "rocks" over their heads then let go of the laces. Encourage kids to practice until they get the hang of it.

# For Further Fun:

● Have a slingshot competition, using crumpled-up newspaper for rocks. See who can sling the paper the farthest, most accurately, and fastest.

● Be sure your kids realize the danger of using their slingshots with real rocks or other heavy objects. Read the story of David and Goliath in 1 Samuel 17 to show how powerful this little instrument can be.

# 2. Joyful Noisemakers

*Kids will make and play inSTRUMents of praise just like David might have used.*

**Theme:** Making music is a good way to praise God.

**Scripture Spotlight 1:** "They sang songs of joy, danced, and played tambourines and stringed instruments" (1 Samuel 18:6b).

**Scripture Spotlight 2:** "Praise him with trumpet blasts; praise him with harps and lyres. Praise him with tambourines and dancing; praise him with stringed instruments and flutes" (Psalm 150:3-4).

**Collect:** Scissors; tempera paint; liquid soap; crayons; glitter; paper scraps; glue; rubber bands; and a variety of boxes such as shoe boxes, cereal boxes taped shut, or tissue boxes

# Here's What to Do:

Before this activity, mix a few teaspoons of liquid soap into your tempera paint. This will help it adhere to boxes with waxy surfaces.

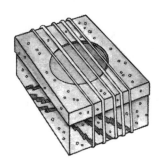

Let each student choose a box. Have each one cut a 4-inch hole in the middle of one of the large sides of the box. Set out tempera paint, crayons, glitter, and paper scraps and allow a few minutes for kids to decorate their boxes anyway they wish. Place the boxes in a sunny place to dry.

While boxes are drying, sing lively praise songs to set the stage for kids to celebrate with their own instruments.

When boxes have dried, distribute five rubber bands to each person. Show kids how to wrap the rubber bands around the boxes so they stretch across the holes. Demonstrate how to strum the instruments lightly to produce a twanging sound. Sing a few more praise songs and encourage kids to make joyful noises with their new instruments.

## For Further Fun:

● To reinforce the theme of praising God with instruments, play instrumental worship music while kids work.

● Have kids work together to sing and play a worship song for their parents.

# 3. Between You and Me

*Kids will make friendship bracelets to give away.*

## Theme: Friends are special gifts from God.

## Scripture Spotlight 1: "Jonathan said to David, 'Go in peace. We have promised by the Lord that we will be friends' " (1 Samuel 20:42a).

## Scripture Spotlight 2: "A friend loves you all the time, and a brother helps in time of trouble" (Proverbs 17:17).

## Collect: Scissors, tape, and various colors of cross-stitch floss cut into 12-inch strands

## Here's What to Do:

Tell children about the special friendship between Jonathan and David. Explain that children will be making friendship bracelets as reminders of the gifts that Jonathan gave to David. Allow each student to choose six strands of cross-stitch floss, two of each color. Have students adjust the strands so that the ends line up evenly then tie a knot at one end. Be sure they leave a 1½-inch tail at that end.

Instruct kids to tape the knotted end to the edge of a table. Lead them through the following instructions, being sure to help those who are having trouble.

1. Arrange the two strands of color A together, the two strands of color B together, and the two strands of color C together. Always use the two strands of each color together.

2. Wrap the strands of color A over then under color B. Pull down on color B as you tighten color A. Then wrap color A over and under color B once more and tighten.

3. Wrap color A over and under color C and tighten. Repeat.

4. Wrap color B over and under color C and tighten. Repeat. Wrap color B over and under color A and tighten Repeat.

5. Wrap color C over and under color A and tighten. Repeat. Wrap color C over and under color B and tighten. Repeat.

## Teacher Tip:

Kids will notice that their cross-stitch floss is made up of six thin strands. Tell kids not to separate the strands but to use all six as one piece.

Have children continue in this sequence until the bracelets are the desired length, then tie all the strands together in one knot. Trim the ends so you leave a 2- to 3-inch tail.

## For Further Fun:
● Use this as an affirmation time. As kids tie the bracelets around partners' wrists, have them each say three things that they like about that person.

● If you have more time, have partners work together on another bracelet to give to someone in the church—another teacher, the pastor, or a friend. As kids work, encourage them to think about what makes a good friend.

● Kids may want to think of a meaning for each color they choose. For example, yellow might symbolize a happy spirit, green could represent a love for nature, and red might show a loving heart. Have kids choose colors that they think symbolize the unique attributes of their partners.

# 4. Serving up a Smile
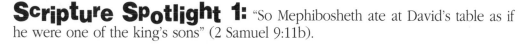
*Kids will make simple serving tables for bringing joy to others.*

**Theme:** We can serve others.

**Scripture Spotlight 1:** "So Mephibosheth ate at David's table as if he were one of the king's sons" (2 Samuel 9:11b).

**Scripture Spotlight 2:** "Be kind and loving to each other, and forgive each other just as God forgave you in Christ" (Ephesians 4:32).

**Collect:** A 1×2-foot rectangle of wood for each student, two 2-inch dowels cut into 1-foot lengths for each student, a hot-glue gun, glue sticks, light sandpaper, acrylic paints, paintbrushes, colored pencils, a damp cloth, and photocopies of the "Table Toppers" handout (p. 46)

## Here's What to Do:
Before this activity, make enough photocopies of the "Table Toppers" handout (p. 46) for each student to have one.

Before you begin, explain that even after Jonathan died, King David was very kind to Jonathan's relatives. Tell children that David invited Jonathan's son Mephibosheth to dine at his table. Explain that kids will be making serving trays or small tables to remind them to serve others, too.

Give each student a 1×2-foot rectangle of wood and a piece of light sandpaper. Set out the acrylic paints, paintbrushes, pencils, and photocopies of the "Table Toppers" handout. Show kids how to sand the wood, going with the grain, so it's smooth and free of splinters. Be sure they sand the top, sides, and bottom then wipe the boards with a damp cloth. Encourage kids to decorate their table tops using paints and the "Table Toppers" stencils or drawing freehand with colored pencils. As children finish, help them use the hot-glue gun to attach the 2-inch dowels at each end. Kids will hold the dowels in place until the hot glue cools.

## For Further Fun:
● Have kids serve each other a snack on their new serving tables. Provide fancy napkins, cups, and a fun treat such as cupcakes or fruit slices to make this a special time of service.

● Have kids collect pretty leaves or cut shapes out of construction paper then lay the items on the wood. Show kids how to decoupage by using foam brushes to apply several layers of shellac.

# Table Toppers

# 5. A Shield Around Me

*Help kids make symbols of God's protection.*

**Theme:** God protects us in difficult times.

**Scripture Spotlight 1:** "The Lord said to David, 'Go! I will certainly hand them over to you' " (2 Samuel 5:19b).

**Scripture Spotlight 2:** "But, Lord, you are my shield, my wonderful God who gives me courage" (Psalm 3:3).

**Collect:** A 2-foot square of foamcore for each student, 7-inch strips of fabric, a glue gun and hot-glue sticks, scissors, glitter, markers, paints, and pencils (optional: colored glue, colored hot-glue sticks, sequins, beads, and foil scraps)

## Here's What to Do:

Give each student a 2-foot square of foamcore. Set out all the other materials and tell kids they'll be creating their own unique shields. Explain that long ago a shield was designed with a family emblem, the colors of a country's flag, or pictures and designs that represented the soldier carrying the shield. Tell children that God protected David in battle just as a shield would. Encourage kids to be creative as they use the materials you've provided to make shields that reflect who they are.

Help students cut the foamcore into their desired shapes. As students are working, go around and attach a 7-inch strip of fabric to the back of each shield. Using the glue gun, place a dot of glue on each end of the fabric, then press it onto the foamcore. Be sure you leave enough loose fabric in the middle for students to grasp.

When students have finished, allow everyone to explain the design on his or her shield.

## For Further Fun:

● Display the shields on the walls of your classroom. Invite parents to try to find their children's shields.

● Make this a family craft by inviting parents to take part. Each family can work together to create a family crest or to design a shield that tells about them.

# Esther

**W**hen Esther became queen, she didn't tell anyone of her Jewish heritage. Soon Haman, a high-ranking official, began plotting to destroy the Jews. A woman of strong character, Esther risked her life to save her people from the evil plot. The king listened and believed her, and the Jews were saved. Jews still celebrate Purim in remembrance of Esther's bravery and wisdom.

**1.** With King Xerxes' approval, Esther was ushered into the palace and took up residence there (Esther 2:17-18). Kids become royalty too when they believe in Jesus. Idea 1, "Paper Palace," will remind kids that they're children of the King of Kings!

**2.** It was a happy day when King Xerxes took action against evil Haman. Esther and Mordecai were victorious, and Haman was executed on the platform that he'd built for Mordecai's death (Esther 7:9-10). It's traditional during the Jewish holiday of Purim to eat three-cornered cookies called Hamantaschen. The cookies are shaped like the three-cornered hat that Haman is believed to have worn. Use Idea 2, "Hamantaschen," to celebrate the victory of good over evil.

**3.** During the retelling of Esther's story at Purim, Jewish children shake gragers, or noisemakers, each time Haman's name is mentioned. Use Idea 3, "Gragers," to help your children learn that it's good to speak up when people are being treated unfairly.

**4.** Mordecai, who warned the king of an assassination plot, was honored with royal robes and a horse. When the Jewish people were saved from Haman's plot, Mordecai wore royal clothes of blue, white, and purple (Esther 8:15). Kids can make royal designs in Idea 4, "Made for Mordecai."

# 1. Paper Palace

*Help kids make a wall of the classroom into a façade of Queen Esther's palace.*

**Theme:** One day we'll see God's kingdom in heaven.

**Scripture Spotlight 1:** "And the king was pleased with Esther...so he put a royal crown on her head and made her queen" (Esther 2:17).

**Scripture Spotlight 2:** "And the street of the city was made of pure gold as clear as glass" (Revelation 21:21b).

**Collect:** Used paper, transparent tape or pushpins, and markers (optional: cardboard wrapping-paper tubes and empty aluminum cans)

## Here's What to Do:

Before class, choose a small wall in your room to "build" on. You'll need a wall to which kids can safely attach transparent tape or pushpins.

Explain that kids will be working together to build the front of a palace. Remind them that Esther went to live in a huge palace when she became queen. Set the used paper and several rolls of transparent tape or several pushpins in the middle of the room. Show kids how to hold the paper vertically, roll the paper so the ends just overlap, then secure it with tape. Have students roll paper for a few minutes until they have a good stock of building materials.

When kids have a good supply of paper rolls, show them how to tape or pin the rolls to the wall vertically to resemble columns of stone. Have kids plan how their palace will look, allowing for a door or gateway and using cardboard wrapping-paper tubes as turrets. When kids have finished, they can stack or flatten empty aluminum cans and use them as decorations.

## For Further Fun:

● Before they roll the paper, have kids lay each sheet against a wall or other rough surface then rub a black or brown crayon across the paper. Each sheet of paper will look textured, adding a nice touch to the palace façade.

● Have kids create the palace on a wall where there's a door. Have each child walk through the "palace door" and be affirmed that he or she is a child of God the King! This could be a great affirmation after each class, sending kids into the world with a sense of who they really are.

# 2. Hamantaschen

*Kids will celebrate Esther's sweet victory with easy-to-make cookies.*

**Theme:** We can rejoice when good wins over evil.

**Scripture Spotlight 1:** "He told them to celebrate those days as days of joyful feasting" (Esther 9:22b).

**Scripture Spotlight 2:** "I pray that victory will come to Israel from Mount Zion!... Then the people of Jacob will rejoice, and the people of Israel will be glad" (Psalm 14:7).

**Collect:** Flour, powdered sugar, margarine, egg yolks, ice water, apricot jam, mixing bowls, a mixing spoon, measuring cups and spoons, rolling pins, and baking sheets

## Here's What to Do:

Explain that kids will be making cookies to celebrate Esther's victory over Haman. Have a volunteer mix 1 stick of softened margarine with 4 tablespoons of powdered sugar. Choose another child to mix in two egg yolks and 3 tablespoons of ice water. The mixture will be lumpy; don't worry if the water doesn't mix in well.

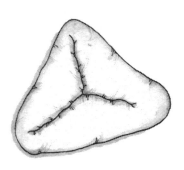

Call on someone to measure out and add 1½ cups of flour. Have the children take turns mixing the dough well. Divide the dough into 12 balls and give one to each child. Have kids roll the dough into 4-inch circles then spread a spoonful of apricot jam in the center. Show them how to fold up and pinch together three edges of the dough into the center of the cookie. Explain that the cookie is a reminder of Haman's three-cornered hat. Be sure they pinch the edges tightly; otherwise the cookies will flatten out while they're baking.

Bake the cookies in a 350-degree oven for 10 to 12 minutes. When done, the cookies should be golden brown.

## For Further Fun:

● Have kids wrap the cookies in colorful tissue paper and present the sweet gifts to each other. As they give the gifts to each other, have kids say, "God gives us sweet victory over evil."

● Plan a joyful feast. Sing praise songs, serve Hamantaschen, and share answers to prayer. Have children share victories that God has given to them or victories that God gave people in the Bible. For example, a child might say, "God gave me victory when I decided to clean my room just as my dad told me to." Then eat the cookies and drink milk or juice to celebrate the sweetness of victory.

# 3. Gragers

*Children will make colorful noisemakers.*

**Theme:** We must speak out against injustice.

**Scripture Spotlight 1:** "Once again Esther spoke to the king. She fell at the king's feet and cried and begged him to stop the evil plan that Haman the Agagite had planned against the Jews" (Esther 8:3).

**Scripture Spotlight 2:** "Don't be afraid. Continue talking to people and don't be quiet" (Acts 18:9b).

**Collect:** Burned-out light bulbs, old newspaper, a large pan or Dutch oven, a spoon, flour, water, sugar, pie tins, measuring cups, tempera paint, and paintbrushes

## Here's What to Do:

NOTE: This craft requires two class sessions.

Before this activity, make an easy papier-mâché paste at home. Mix 2 cups of flour with ½ cup of sugar in a large pan or Dutch oven. Stir in warm water until a paste forms. Then stir in ½ gallon of warm water. Stir over moderate heat until the mixture boils and becomes thick and clear. Then remove from heat and stir in 2 cups of cold water.

Place a few cups of the paste in several pie tins. Have children tear long, thin newspaper strips and pull the strips through the paste. Have children cover burned-out light bulbs with four or five layers of wet newspaper strips then set them in a warm, sunny place to dry until your next class.

When the newspaper is completely dry, have children hit the gragers against the floor or a table top to break the glass inside. Caution children not to break through the papier-mâché layer, or glass will spill out. Then have children paint their noisemakers with bright colors.

## For Further Fun:

● Act out the story of Esther, just as Jewish people do during Purim. Choose children to play Esther, King Xerxes, Haman, and Mordecai. Have the rest of the children be Jews. Read the story and have the children act it out. Have the Jews shake their gragers when Haman's name is mentioned.

● Have kids use their gragers as worship instruments. Choose an upbeat song such as "I Will Celebrate" and allow kids to accent the music with their gragers.

# 4. Made for Mordecai

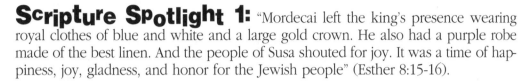

*Kids will make one-of-a-kind wrapping paper.*

**Theme:** God rewards those who serve him.

**Scripture Spotlight 1:** "Mordecai left the king's presence wearing royal clothes of blue and white and a large gold crown. He also had a purple robe made of the best linen. And the people of Susa shouted for joy. It was a time of happiness, joy, gladness, and honor for the Jewish people" (Esther 8:15-16).

**Scripture Spotlight 2:** "The Son of Man will come again with his Father's glory and with his angels. At that time, he will reward them for what they have done" (Matthew 16:27).

**Collect:** Purple, blue, and gold tempera or acrylic paint; old rags or socks; pie tins; large sheets of coated paper; and newspaper

## Here's What to Do:

Before this activity, divide the tempera or acrylic paint into several pie tins. Set the tins in groupings of three (one of each color) all around the room. Place at least three rags or socks and a stack of newspaper in each of these painting areas as well.

Distribute large sheets of coated paper and have kids form trios near the paint. Instruct kids to generously spread the newspaper on the floor in their work areas. Help kids tie a knot in the middle of each of their rags or socks. Then show them how to grasp the ends of the rags, roll the knots in the paint, then roll the knots along their papers to make designs. Kids can alternate colors to make their own unique patterns.

When kids are satisfied with their designs, have them lay the papers in a sunny place to dry.

## For Further Fun:

● Have kids make simple gifts (perhaps some described in this book!) for their parents. Gather students together and help them wrap the gifts with their unique wrapping paper.

● Decorate gift bags or boxes in the same way.

# Jonah

**W**hen God told Jonah to go to Nineveh and warn the people there that God would destroy their city if they didn't change their ways, Jonah didn't argue. He immediately got up and headed in the opposite direction as fast as he could! It took a storm, a near drowning, and three days inside a large fish to change Jonah's mind and turn him toward Nineveh (Jonah 1–2). Kids today can relate to Jonah's reaction to God's commands. Often they'd like to turn and run from difficulties or uncomfortable situations. The ideas in this section can help kids learn from Jonah's experience and realize that obeying God is always the best decision.

**1.** After God spoke to Jonah, the first thing Jonah did was to hop aboard a ship headed in the other direction (Jonah 1:3). This unfortunate vessel was headed for stormy weather, though! In Idea 1, "Sailing Away From God," your students can build a ship and act out the storm that got Jonah's attention.

**2.** God used great creativity when he sent a large fish to swallow Jonah (Jonah 1:17). Though we'll never know what it was like inside the belly of that fish, kids can experience in Idea 2, "A Whale of a Tale," some of what Jonah might have gone through.

**3.** Although Jonah went through uncomfortable circumstances, God never left his side. This story can remind kids that God is always with them, even when they sin and turn from God. Idea 3, "Chasing Away Fear," will give kids a chance to make something that will remind them of God's presence.

**4.** We can imagine Jonah feeling lonely and lost—perhaps even doomed—inside the belly of the great fish. But he cried out to God, knowing that God cared and would listen to him (Jonah 2). In our stressed-out society, kids often feel lost in the shuffle, so it's important that they know of God's love and protection. Idea 4, "On the Inside," will show kids that even when they feel invisible to others, God sees and cares for them.

**5.** Although most of us remember Jonah for his escapades inside a fish, he did a wonderful work when he took the message of God's love and power to the people of Nineveh. Jonah's words and God's great power saved the people from destruction! Kids can follow Jonah's example by using Idea 5, "Jonah Necklaces," to tell others of God's love, protection, and power.

# 1. Sailing Away From God

*Kids will work cooperatively to create a ship.*

**Theme:** We can't run from God.

**Scripture Spotlight 1:** "But Jonah got up to run away from the Lord by going to Tarshish" (Jonah 1:3a).

**Scripture Spotlight 2:** "Where can I run from you? If I go up to the heavens, you are there. If I lie down in the grave, you are there. If I rise with the sun in the east and settle in the west beyond the sea, even there you would guide me" (Psalm 139:7b-10a).

**Collect:** Two large pieces of foamcore (each 8 to 10 feet long) or an appliance box, paint shirts, tempera paint, paintbrushes, chairs, an old bedsheet, dowels or a yardstick, pencils, scissors, fishing line, masking tape, and a box fan (optional: squirt guns and blue crepe paper streamers)

## Here's What to Do:

Before you gather, set up three centers around the room. Place a large piece of foamcore (8 to 10 feet long) or one side of an appliance box, scissors, tempera paint, paintbrushes, and paint shirts at one center labeled "boat building." Set another large piece of foamcore (or appliance box), paint, paintbrushes, paint shirts, and chairs at another center labeled "wave making." Finally, place an old bedsheet, dowels or a yardstick, and scissors at a third center labeled "sail stitching."

Explain each center to the children and let them go to the centers of their choice. The group at the "boat building" center will paint a ship on the foamcore or cardboard. Students may want to choose an artist to sketch the boat in pencil, then work together to paint it. When the boat is finished, have students cut it out.

At the "wave making" area, students will paint swirling ocean waves on the foamcore or cardboard. Allow students to choose whether they'll make one long line of waves or several rows. When the waves are completed, have students cut them out then line up four chairs along the wall with the chair backs toward the room. They can work with the boat builders to attach their foamcore pieces to the chair backs, using masking tape.

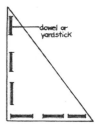

At the "sail stitching" center students will make a sail from an old bedsheet. Have one student cut the sheet diagonally from top to bottom. Show an older student how to poke small holes along the long, vertical edges, using scissors. Have three children hold the corners of the sail while another student weaves the dowel or yardstick in and out of the holes. Do the same on the smaller horizontal edge.

String a length of fishing line through the holes in the sail, then tape it to the ceiling above the row of chairs. Have kids tie the lower end of the fishing line to one of the chair backs.

Turn the box fan to its high setting to create wind while children "ride" on the ship by kneeling on the chairs.

Option: Tape blue crepe paper streamers to the box fan to create more "waves." For more realistic waves, have students spray water into the wind with squirt guns.

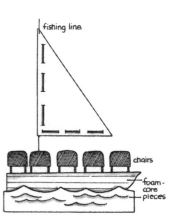

## For Further Fun:

● Bring squares of craft netting and a box of fish crackers. Have children go two or three at a time onto the boat and lower their nets. Position other children with five-ounce paper cups full of fish crackers to place into the nets. This is a fun and creative way to catch a snack!

● Invite another class to watch as students use the ship to act out the story of Jonah. If you use both this idea and the previous one, kids will really experience Jonah's adventure!

# 2. A Whale of a Tale

*Kids will discover what it might have been like inside the big fish.*

**Theme:** Jonah prays inside the belly of the great fish.

**Scripture Spotlight 1:** "The Lord caused a big fish to swallow Jonah, and Jonah was inside the fish three days and three nights" (Jonah 1:17).

**Scripture Spotlight 2:** "When my life had almost gone, I remembered the Lord. I prayed to you, and you heard my prayers in your Holy Temple" (Jonah 2:7).

**Collect:** A 12-foot square of landscaping plastic (larger classes may need a larger square of plastic), duct tape, paint shirts, gray and blue tempera paints mixed with glue, sponges, paper plates, and a box fan

## Here's What to Do:

Lay the landscaping plastic on the floor in the center of your room.

Form two groups. Tell kids that they're going to help make a whale they can sit inside! Pour tempera paint onto the paper plates and have one group use the sponges to paint the top of the plastic. Instruct the other group to tape down the edges of the plastic with the duct tape. Be sure this group doesn't stretch the plastic to its full 12 feet. Have them leave the plastic fairly loose in the middle. This may work best if one student cuts long lengths of tape while others use them to tape the edges of the plastic to the floor. Instruct this group to tape the plastic onto the floor on two sides. They'll need to tape one end of the plastic securely to the edges of the box fan and tape the opposite end to the floor, leaving an opening for a mouth where everyone can crawl into the belly of the "whale."

When the paint is dry and the plastic is securely taped down, turn on the fan and allow the whale to "grow." When there appears to be enough space inside, have students crawl one by one inside the whale.

## For Further Fun:

● Have kids tape green crepe paper streamers to the box fan. The streamers can represent seaweed.

● Take fish sticks into the whale for a fun snack.

● Allow each student the chance to sit alone inside the whale for three minutes. Talk about how Jonah must have felt being alone for three days.

# 3. Chasing Away Fear

*Kids will make Jonah medallions.*

**Theme:** If God is with us, we don't have to fear.

**Scripture Spotlight 1:** "But you saved me from the pit of death, Lord my God" (Jonah 2:6b).

**Scripture Spotlight 2:** "If God is with us, no one can defeat us" (Romans 8:31).

**Collect:** Lids from frozen-juice cans (the kind that come off with plastic strips), pencils, one nail for each student, hammers, blocks of scrap wood, acrylic paints, paint shirts, paintbrushes, colored felt, and a 20-inch leather lace for each child

## Here's What to Do:

Give each child a pencil and a can lid. Instruct kids to draw simple designs on their can lids. Explain that kids will be making medallions for certain attributes such as faithfulness, kindness, helpfulness, and patience. Encourage children to make their designs symbolize attributes, such as a heart for love, a hand for helpfulness, a smile for cheerfulness, or a cross for someone who loves Jesus. Then show them how to lay the lids on blocks of scrap wood and to nail holes in the lids to outline the designs. The nail holes should be about ¼ inch apart. When they've outlined their designs, kids may paint over them with acrylic paints.

While the paint is drying, have kids trace around the can lids on pieces of colored felt. Show them how to cut out the felt circles and glue them to the back of the lids—the side the nails have been punched through. This will cover any sharp edges and allow a bit of color to peek through the holes. Then have kids use the nails to make holes in the top of their medallions and tie leather laces through them.

## For Further Fun:

● Have an awards ceremony and present each child with his or her medallion. Award children for different attributes such as faithfulness, kindness, helpfulness, and patience.

● Kids can use this same method to make sun catchers for their windows at home. Omit the felt backing and hang them in windows so the sun shines through. These can be reminders that God wants to let his light shine through us.

# 4. On the Inside

*Kids can see Jonah in the belly of the fish.*

**Theme:** God surrounded Jonah with protection.

**Scripture Spotlight 1:** "The Lord caused a big fish to swallow Jonah and Jonah was inside the fish three days and three nights" (Jonah 1:17).

**Scripture Spotlight 2:** "But the Lord is faithful and will give you strength and will protect you from the Evil One" (2 Thessalonians 3:3).

**Collect:** 10-inch balloons, 12-inch strands of yarn, pre-mixed plaster of Paris, paper plates, wax paper, 2-inch squares of poster board or old cereal boxes, crayons or markers, 7-inch lengths of string, pencils, construction paper, glue, and scissors

## Here's What to Do:

Give each child a 2-inch square of poster board and have him or her draw a person on it. Have kids cut out their drawings then tie them to the end of 7-inch lengths of string.

Distribute 10-inch balloons and have kids squeeze their poster board people into the balloons then blow up the balloons. Help kids tie off the balloons so that a few inches of the string hangs out.

Pour a few cups of the wet plaster of Paris onto several paper plates. Show kids

how to dip the 12-inch strands of yarn into the plaster of Paris and wrap it evenly around the balloons. Have kids continue until most of each balloon is covered with yarn. Allow balloons to dry on squares of wax paper in a sunny place. Tie the string to a few of the plaster-yarn pieces. When the plaster is completely dry, have kids use the tip of a pencil to pop their balloons then carefully remove them from the inside of the plaster "casts." Be sure they leave the cardboard people on the inside.

Have kids cut fins, eyes, and a spout of water from construction paper and glue them on the plaster whale. Kids can hang their whales (Jonah and all!) from the ceiling.

## For Further Fun:
● Create one of these whales but have kids write affirming notes to each other and slip these inside the balloon. Then give kids chopsticks and have them each pull out a note and read it aloud.

# 5. Jonah Necklaces
*Kids will make a wearable project they can use to tell others about God.*

**Theme:** We can tell others the good news.

**Scripture Spotlight 1:** "After Jonah had entered the city and walked for one day, he preached to the people, saying, 'After forty days, Nineveh will be destroyed!' The people of Nineveh believed God" (Jonah 3:4-5a).

**Scripture Spotlight 2:** "So go and make followers of all people in the world...Teach them to obey everything that I have taught you, and I will be with you always, even until the end of this age" (Matthew 28:19-20).

**Collect:** Leather laces and one craft bead of each of the following colors for each child: gray, red, blue, white, green, yellow

## Here's What to Do:
Have children string their colored craft beads onto leather laces in this order:
Gray—People of Nineveh had *sinned.*
Red—God told Jonah to tell the people to *stop* sinning.
Blue—Jonah disobeyed God. The men threw him into the *ocean.*
White—The people of Nineveh repented. God made their hearts *spotless.*
Green—God gave the people eternal life. He also gave Jonah a *leafy shelter.*
Yellow—Jonah helped the people learn about *heaven.*
Have kids practice telling the story, using the beaded necklace.

## For Further Fun:
● Children can use these necklaces as tools to tell their friends the story of Jonah.

# The New Testament

# Jesus' Birth

**B**irthdays are fun times of celebration for children. But there's only one person whose birthday is celebrated all around the world—Jesus Christ! For those who know Jesus, the celebration of Christmas brings deep feelings of wonder, joy, and love. The glorious birth of Jesus brings a message of hope to all those who hear and believe.

**1.** An angel of the Lord appeared to Mary and Joseph with unbelievable news (Matthew 1:20-23): God's very own Son was to be born of Mary, who was a virgin. Now more than at any other time in their lives, Mary and Joseph needed to trust God to care for them. Because they trusted, they were able to obey God completely. Use Idea 1, "Away in a Manger," to help children discover that trusting God makes life sweet.

**2.** God led Magi from the east by placing a special star in the sky that guided them to Jesus (Matthew 2:2). Kids can create their own special stars in Idea 2, "Star Light, Star Bright."

**3.** The visiting Magi had traveled a long way to worship Jesus. These visitors brought Jesus special gifts of gold, frankincense, and myrrh. Idea 3, "Fit for a King," shows children that they too can give Jesus their best.

**4.** Although Jesus was born in a humble stable, a host of angels announced his birth to nearby shepherds. As they sculpt angels from aluminum foil in Idea 4, "Heavenly Hosts," kids can imagine how the heavenly choir must have sounded.

**5.** After hearing that Jesus was born, many came to honor and worship him (Matthew 2:9-11). Use Idea 5, "Joyful Noises," to help kids experience what it means to worship Jesus.

# 1. Away in a Manger

*Kids will make edible mangers that will remind them of Jesus' lowly birthplace.*

**Theme:** We can trust God to care for us.

**Scripture Spotlight 1:** "When Joseph woke up, he did what the Lord's angel had told him to do" (Matthew 1:24a).

**Scripture Spotlight 2:** "Trust the Lord with all your heart, and don't depend on your own understanding. Remember the Lord in all you do, and he will give you success" (Proverbs 3:5-6).

**Collect:** Marshmallow crème, fat pretzel sticks, graham crackers, frosted shredded wheat cereal, and paper plates

## Here's What to Do:

Set all the materials in the middle of the table and give each child a paper plate. Have kids begin by breaking up several pieces of the frosted shredded wheat cereal and putting it in piles on their plates.

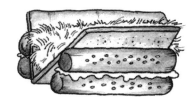

Give children each four pretzel sticks and instruct them to put their pretzels into pairs. Then show kids how to stick each pair together with marshmallow crème. Show them how to lean one-fourth of a graham cracker on each of the pretzel pairs to form mangers. Have kids glue the crackers to the pretzel pairs, using the marshmallow crème. Then allow students to fill the mangers with the shredded-cereal "hay." Before kids enjoy their manger treats, have everyone sing "Away in a Manger" to remember the lowly place where Jesus—a king—was born.

## For Further Fun:

● Pairs or trios can work together to make stables, using these same materials. Graham crackers can make walls, pretzel sticks can hold up the roof, and the shredded wheat makes wonderful (and tasty) hay!

# 2. Starlight, Star Bright

*Kids will make mobiles of shiny stars.*

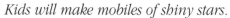

**Theme:** God led people to worship baby Jesus.

## Scripture Spotlight 1: "When the wise men saw the star, they were filled with joy…and they bowed down and worshiped him" (Matthew 2:10a, 11a).

## Scripture Spotlight 2: "Some shepherds were in the fields nearby watching their sheep. Then an angel of the Lord stood before them. The glory of the Lord was shining around them" (Luke 2:8-9a).

**Collect:** Gold or silver wrapping paper, pencils, scissors, string, rulers, copies of the "Starlight" handout (p. 61), tape, and sturdy paper plates

## Here's What to Do:

Before class, cut the wrapping paper into 4-inch squares. Make enough copies of the "Starlight" handout (p. 61) for each child to have one. Set all supplies in the middle of the room.

Distribute the "Starlight" handouts and show kids how to cut out the star patterns and trace them onto the squares of shiny paper. Have kids each make 12 stars, in any combination of styles, then set the stars aside.

Form pairs and give each pair a ruler, scissors, and two 8½-foot sections of string. Instruct pairs to work together and cut each piece of string into 12 segments beginning with a 3-inch length and cutting each segment 1 inch longer than the previous one. For example, kids will cut a 3-inch length, a 4-inch length, a 5-inch length, and so on from each string. When pairs have cut 12 segments for each partner, instruct them to use a sharp pencil to poke a small hole in the top of each star then tie the string through each star. Have kids lay out their string in order from shortest to longest.

Have each child cut out the inside of a paper plate, leaving a ring with a 1½-inch rim. Say: **Imagine this ring is a clock. Place a dot at each number from one to 12. Then poke your scissors through the dots to make small holes. You'll hang your stars from these holes.**

Help students poke their strings through the holes then tape the end of their strings to the back of the paper plate rings. Be sure kids hang their stars in order from shortest to longest. When kids finish, show them how to cut four 8-inch lengths of string and attach them to the 12, 3, 6, and 9 o'clock sections of the rings. Kids can then tie the four strings together to make hangers for their star mobiles.

## For Further Fun:

● Have kids cut out figures to represent the wise men, Jesus, Mary, Joseph, and the shepherds and make a mobile of a Nativity scene.

● Allow kids to write on each star things they're thankful for as a reminder of the good things God has given them.

# 3. Fit for a King

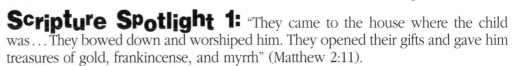

*Students will make sweet-smelling sachets.*

**Theme:** We should give Jesus our best.

**Scripture Spotlight 1:** "They came to the house where the child was…They bowed down and worshiped him. They opened their gifts and gave him treasures of gold, frankincense, and myrrh" (Matthew 2:11).

**Scripture Spotlight 2:** "You must bring the best of the firstfruits of your land to the Holy Tent of the Lord your God" (Exodus 23:19a).

**Collect:** Brightly colored fabric cut into 5½-inch circles, vanilla beans, whole cloves, dried basil, measuring spoons, sealable plastic bags, hammers, rubber bands, scissors, and 6-inch lengths of ribbon

## Here's What to Do:

Form trios and explain that kids will be making sachets to represent the sweet-smelling gifts the wise men brought to Jesus. Give each group a hammer (a large block will work just as well), a sealable plastic bag, a vanilla bean, a tablespoon of whole cloves, and four teaspoons of dried basil.

Have kids place all of the spices inside the bags, seal them, and take turns hitting them with the hammers. Instruct kids to crush the vanilla and cloves until they're broken into many small pieces. When the spices are sufficiently crushed, have each trio divide its spices into three equal parts and place one part in the center of each one of the fabric circles. Be sure kids place the spices on the *backside* of the fabric.

Have kids gather the fabric around the spices and secure it with a rubber band. Then allow kids to choose colors of ribbon that match their fabric and tie the fabric tightly with their ribbon. Once the ribbon is in place, students may cut away the rubber bands.

## For Further Fun:

● Older kids can sew a short basting stitch about 1¼ inches from the edge of the fabric. Show them how to pull the thread so it gathers the fabric tightly. They can then sew a few stitches through the gathered part to seal the sachet.

● Kids can make other scented sachets using cinnamon sticks, dried rose petals, dried citrus peel, or commercial potpourri.

# Starlight

Have each child cut out a star and practice folding along the dotted lines. Children may then use the cutouts as stencils to make stars for their mobiles.

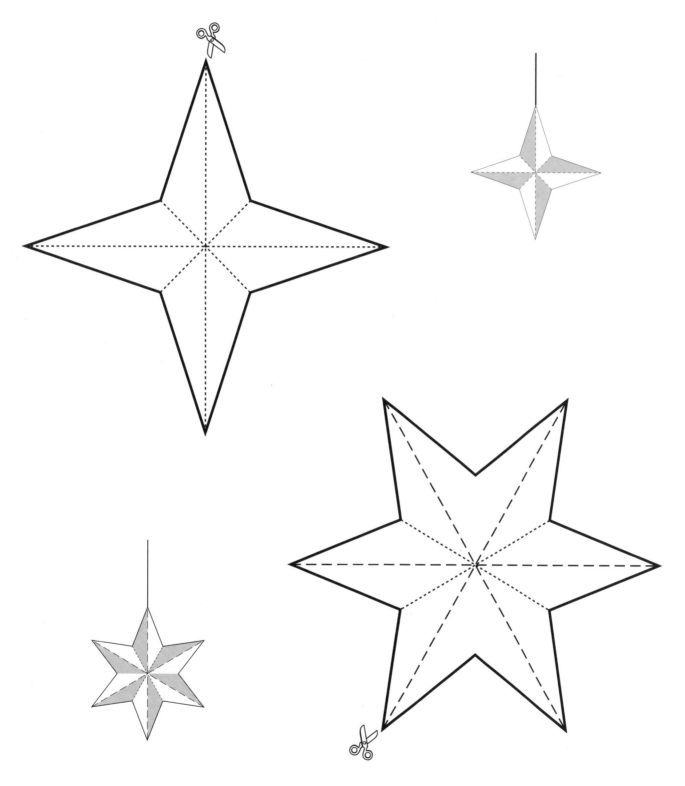

# 4. Heavenly Hosts

*Students will turn aluminum foil into shiny angels.*

**Theme:** The angels announced Jesus' birth.

**Scripture Spotlight 1:** "Then a very large group of angels from heaven joined the first angel, praising God" (Luke 2:13).

**Scripture Spotlight 2:** "The angel said to her, 'Don't be afraid, Mary; God has shown you his grace' " (Luke 1:30).

**Collect:** Aluminum foil

## Here's What to Do:

Give each student a large sheet of aluminum foil (approximately 2 feet long). Show kids how to crumple and mold the foil. Have kids mold their foil into the form of an angel. Encourage kids to be creative and make their own unique angels.

## For Further Fun:

● Kids can use more foil to make a whole Nativity scene! You may want to have groups make them then give these scenes away to other classes.

# 5. Joyful Noises

*Kids will make instruments to help them worship Jesus.*

**Theme:** We should joyfully worship Jesus.

**Scripture Spotlight 1:** "Then a very large group of angels from heaven joined the first angel, praising God" (Luke 2:13).

**Scripture Spotlight 2:** "Serve the Lord with joy; come before him with singing" (Psalm 100:2).

**Collect:** Paper plates, spoons, dry beans, a stapler, curling ribbon, bows, a hole punch, and markers (optional: wrapping paper, old keys, jingle bells, hard Christmas candies, candy canes, and glitter glue)

## Here's What to Do:

Set out all of the materials and explain that children will be making Christmas tambourines. Allow children to create their own unique instruments with the materials provided. Encourage kids with the following ideas:

● Fold a paper plate in half, pour in several spoonfuls of dry beans, then staple the edges shut.

● Place two paper plates together and punch holes around the edge. Weave a length of curling ribbon through the holes, leaving a small space and then pouring in hard Christmas candies or dry beans. Finish weaving and tie off the ribbon.

● Punch holes around the edge of a paper plate, then tie jingle bells or old keys to each hole. Kids can tap this tambourine with a candy cane "drumstick."

Allow children to decorate their instruments with ribbon, bows, bits of wrapping paper, glitter glue, or other items you've brought in.

## For Further Fun:

● Have a Christmas carol sing, allowing children to request their favorites. Encourage kids to accent the singing with their instruments.

# Jesus Calls His Followers

*I*t began with a simple command: "Come follow me" (Mark 1:17a). Simon, Andrew, James, and John obeyed, and their lives were changed forever. They embarked upon an amazing adventure as the closest companions of the Son of God. Later, Jesus called 72 people to go out in his name (Luke 10:1-12). These 72 returned with joy, having witnessed God's power at work. Children today can discover that same excitement when they choose to serve and follow Jesus. Use the ideas in this section to help children experience what it means to follow our Lord.

**1.** Mark 1:17 contains one of Jesus' most important commands: "Follow me." In that context it was directed to Simon, Andrew, James, and John, but it remains a timeless call to discipleship. Use Idea 1, "Followers' Footprints," to help children understand that they too can follow Jesus.

**2.** Although the fishermen may have been confused about what it meant to "fish for people," they did just that. The disciples faithfully fished for people as they spread the gospel of Christ. Idea 2, "Something Fishy," will allow children to make a fish-shaped snack that will remind them that they can "catch" other people with Jesus' love.

**3.** Jesus sent the 72 out in pairs with a message of peace. He gave them specific directions to share a blessing of peace with each household where they stayed. Jesus also taught that his followers should be peacemakers. Use Idea 3, "Peace to You," to help children realize that a big part of fishing for people is sharing God's peace in loving, caring ways.

**4.** Jesus sent out the 72 with strict instructions not to take money or extra clothing with them. Jesus even warned them that he was sending them out as lambs among wolves. Yet they returned to Jesus with joy! Children are naturally joyful, and Idea 4, "Hung up on Smiles," lets them celebrate the joy of being Jesus' followers.

**5.** Jesus gave his followers support that no other teacher could—he gave them power over their enemies. "Nothing will hurt you," Jesus said (Luke 10:19b). Idea 5, "It's Powerful," will provide children with a reminder of God's power.

# 1. Followers' Footprints

*Kids will decorate T-shirts with painted footprints.*

**Theme:** Jesus calls us to be his followers.

**Scripture Spotlight 1:** "Jesus said to them, 'Come follow me' " (Mark 1:17a).

**Scripture Spotlight 2:** "The person who follows me . . . will have the light that gives life" (John 8:12b).

**Collect:** Plain white T-shirts (pre-washed), scissors, cardboard, markers, masking tape, clothespins, two or three colors of liquid fabric paint, a chair, pie tins, newspaper, a large basin of warm soapy water, paper towels, and bottles of puffy paint

## Here's What to Do:

Before this activity, cut cardboard rectangles that will fit inside the T-shirts and prevent paint from soaking through from the front to the back. The cardboard will also give a solid surface for applying paint. Cover an area of the floor with plenty of newspaper. Set up a washing area nearby by placing paper towels on the floor under a basin of warm soapy water. If weather allows, do this craft outside on the grass, then hose off children's feet for easy cleanup. Pour a thin layer of liquid fabric paint into each pie tin.

Distribute plain white T-shirts and have children print their names on the tags or on pieces of masking tape to temporarily stick to the shirts. Then show kids how to gather the back of the shirts so the front is pulled taut against the cardboard insert. Help them use clothespins to hold the shirts this way. Instruct kids to remove their shoes and socks and form a circle around the newspaper-covered area. Explain that kids will take turns sitting on the chair, placing their T-shirt in front of them, and carefully dipping their feet into the paint. Then they will step firmly on their T-shirts to make footprints. The children may choose to use one or more colors of paint.

As kids finish, move their T-shirts aside and have them wipe their feet with paper towels then step into the basin of soapy water. Provide more paper towels for drying.

When the footprints have dried, allow children to use puffy paint to write their names or messages such as "I follow Jesus!" on their shirts.

Let the paint on the T-shirts dry completely before you remove the cardboard insert and clothespins.

## For Further Fun:

● Have kids decorate plain canvas baseball caps or white canvas shoes to match.

● While kids have their shoes off, have them make a large banner on newsprint. Older kids can work together to write, "Come follow me" (Mark 1:17a), and younger kids can decorate the lettering. Have each child walk across the banner with paint-covered bare feet. You can hang the banner in your classroom or in the front of your church.

# 2. Something Fishy

*Kids will make colorful fish-shaped candies.*

**Theme:** We can "catch" others who may become followers of Jesus, too.

**Scripture Spotlight 1:** "I will make you fish for people" (Mark 1:17b).

**Scripture Spotlight 2:** "Jesus said to his followers, 'Go everywhere in the world, and tell the Good News to everyone'" (Mark 16:15).

**Collect:** Aluminum foil; translucent hard candies in a variety of solid colors (Jolly Rancher candies work well); small plastic bags; a mallet or hammer; greased cookie sheets; toothpicks; and thread, ribbon, or string

## Here's What to Do:

Before class, use a mallet or hammer to crush each color of hard candy in a separate plastic bag. If you have older children, allow them to do this. Preheat an oven to 300 degrees.

Give each child a sheet of aluminum foil and demonstrate how to form the foil into a fish-shaped mold about 3 inches long. Have children place their molds on greased cookie sheets. Be sure the cookie sheets aren't bent, or the candy will run outside of the mold. Allow kids to select one or two colors of crushed candy to sprinkle into their foil shapes. Mixing colors will create a marbled look. Be sure kids fill the area inside their molds evenly but not too thickly.

Bake the fish shapes in the preheated oven for five minutes. As soon as the cookie sheets are removed from the oven, allow kids to use toothpicks to poke a hole in the top center of each melted fish shape. Encourage children to use caution in handling their hot molds. Leave the toothpicks in the molds until the candy hardens slightly.

While the candies are hardening, have children cut lengths of string, thread, or ribbon to make hangers for their fish shapes. When the fish shapes have cooled, help children peel away the foil molds and thread and tie their hangers. Some children may wish to hang the candy shapes in a bright window as sun catchers; others may want to enjoy their snacks right away!

## For Further Fun:

● Use a variety of metal cookie cutters to create several different sun-catcher designs.

● Have kids print Mark 1:17a on slips of paper and tie the papers to the hangers. Kids can give these away, sharing their faith with others.

# 3. Peace to You

*Children will design doorknob hangers to share God's peace.*

**Theme:** God asks us to share peace with others.

**Scripture Spotlight 1:** "Before you go into a house, say, 'Peace be with this house'" (Luke 10:5).

**Scripture Spotlight 2:** "Live in peace with each other" (Romans 12:16a).

**Collect:** Photocopies of the "Peace" handout (p. 67), white crayons, watercolors, paintbrushes, small bowls of water, and scissors

## Here's What to Do:

Before class, photocopy the "Peace" handout (p. 67) on heavy paper so you have one copy per child.

Distribute copies of the "Peace" handout and have children cut out their doorknob hangers, including the slits for slipping the hangers over doorknobs. Instruct them to use the white crayons to color in the letters of the word "peace." Once all of their letters have been colored in, have each student paint over the entire paper with watercolors. Encourage students to swirl different colors and let the colors run together. The crayon in the letters will resist the paint and remain white, while the rest of the hanger absorbs the color.

When the paint has dried, instruct students to print their names on the back of their hangers. Encourage kids to tell whose doors they'll place their hangers on.

Have the children practice saying the phrase from the hangers so they can share it with the people who receive them.

## For Further Fun:

● Have each child make another door hanger. When these hangers are dry, send children out in pairs to place the hangers on other classroom doors.

# 4. Hung Up on Smiles

*Children will design creative puppets to celebrate the joy of following Jesus.*

**Theme:** Following Jesus is a joy.

**Scripture Spotlight 1:** "When the seventy-two came back, they were very happy and said, 'Lord, even the demons obeyed us when we used your name!'" (Luke 10:17).

**Scripture Spotlight 2:** "Be full of joy in the Lord always" (Philippians 4:4a).

**Collect:** Nylon hose, wire hangers, fabric scraps, yarn, construction paper, puffy paint, scissors, glue, rubber bands, and ribbon

## Here's What to Do:

Before class, cut the legs off the nylon hose (unless you're using knee-highs). You'll need one hose leg per child.

Distribute wire hangers and help children stretch theirs into circles. Then give each child a nylon hose leg and show him or her how to pull the toe section of the hose over the hanger. Have kids pull the hose legs tight then use rubber bands to secure them at the base of the circles. Provide lengths of ribbon for kids to tie around the rubber bands.

Allow students to use fabric scraps, yarn, construction paper, and puffy paint to make happy faces on the stretched hose.

## For Further Fun:

● Children may use their puppets as masks, performing a short skit or play about Jesus' disciples.

# Peace

● Before children glue items on their puppets, set out pre-cut fabric scraps with masking tape rolls on the back. Children may choose items and create certain faces, then pull them off and try new ones.

# 5. It's POWerful

*Help kids decorate light-switch plates to hang in their bedrooms.*

**Theme:** Jesus gives us power and strength to do his work.

**Scripture Spotlight 1:** "Listen, I have given you power...that is greater than the enemy has. So nothing will hurt you" (Luke 10:19).

**Scripture Spotlight 2:** "I can do all things through Christ, because he gives me strength" (Philippians 4:13).

**Collect:** Plain light-switch plates (from a hardware or craft store), fluorescent or glow-in-the-dark paints, paintbrushes, and newspaper

## Here's What to Do:

Cover your work space with newspaper and place the fluorescent or glow-in-the-dark paints in the middle. Give each child a light-switch plate and instruct kids to design light-switch plates to hang in their bedrooms. Encourage kids to create designs that will remind them of God's power.

When kids finish, set the plates aside to dry. Have kids take them home with notes of simple instructions for installation: Unscrew the current light-switch plate and replace it with the decorated one, using the same screws.

## For Further Fun:

● Purchase blank wooden switch plates at a craft store. Cut small fish shapes from a sponge and have kids sponge-paint fish shapes onto the switch plates.

# Sermon on the Mount (Part 1)

**T**he pursuit of happiness has become a national pastime. We spend money on cars, clothes, vacations, gadgets, and seminars that we hope will bring us lasting joy. While these may bring about a temporary *sense of happiness, Matthew 5:1-16 outlines God's prescription for enduring joy. Use the ideas in this section to help students learn how to find real happiness God's way!*

**1.** When Jesus called his followers the salt of the earth (Matthew 5:13), he wanted them to realize that they could make a difference in the world. Without seasoning, food is tasteless; without Christians, the world would be in darkness. Idea 1, "Salty Servers," will remind kids that their faith can make a difference.

**2.** In Matthew 5:14, Jesus calls us the light of the world. Idea 2, "Lighten Up," will encourage kids to boldly demonstrate Jesus' love in their lives.

**3.** We probably don't need to be reminded that other people sometimes lie, insult us, and hurt us (Matthew 5:11). We *do* need Christ's reminder and encouragement to "shine" in these difficult circumstances (Matthew 5:16). Use Idea 3, "Shine On," to encourage kids to live in such a way that others see the difference Jesus makes in their lives.

**4.** Jesus wants his followers to stand out from the crowd. When we live for Jesus, others notice and God receives praise (Matthew 5:16). Use Idea 4, "Splatter Strings," to challenge kids to stand out from the crowd and joyfully live for Christ.

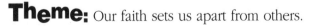

# 1. Salty Servers

*Kids will use colored salt and their creativity to paint beautiful pictures.*

**Theme:** Our faith sets us apart from others.

**Scripture Spotlight 1:** "You are the salt of the earth" (Matthew 5:13a).

**Scripture Spotlight 2:** "If people say they have faith, but do nothing, their faith is worth nothing" (James 2:14).

**Collect:** Sealable plastic bags, measuring cups, colored sidewalk chalk (bright colors work best), coarse salt or rock salt, wooden blocks, aluminum pie tins, plastic spoons, paper, glue, and pencils

## Here's What to Do:

Form pairs and give each pair a piece of colored sidewalk chalk and a sealable plastic bag. Instruct pairs to place the chalk into their bags, seal the bags tightly, then crush the chalk with wooden blocks. Then pour two cups of coarse salt or rock salt into each bag and have partners take turns shaking and squishing the bag for about three to five minutes or until all of the salt is colored. While children are coloring the salt, talk about all the uses for salt, such as flavoring popcorn, making icy sidewalks safer, or making homemade ice cream. Explain that Jesus called his followers salt and light for the world.

Have kids pour their colored salt into pie tins so there's a different color of salt in each tin. Place a spoon in each tin and place the tins in the middle of a table. Have children gather around the table to create their pictures.

Give each child a sheet of paper and a pencil. Allow about three minutes for kids to sketch simple pictures or designs. When students have finished, show them how to spread a thin layer of glue on each picture then sprinkle colored salt on it. Have each child spread glue on sections of his or her picture rather than on the whole paper at once. When the glue dries, have children shake excess salt back into the appropriate pie tin.

## For Further Fun:

● When the glue has dried completely, lightly spray the pictures with water to make them sparkle.

● To "trample" your salt pictures, wait until they dry, then place the pictures between two sheets of newspaper. Allow kids to roll over their pictures with a rolling pin. This crushes the salt and gives the pictures a softer look.

# 2. Lighten Up

*Kids will create stained-glass candleholders.*

**Theme:** We can be lights in a dark world.

**Scripture Spotlight 1:** "You are the light that gives light to the world" (Matthew 5:14a).

**Scripture Spotlight 2:** "Do everything without complaining or arguing...Shine like stars in the dark world" (Philippians 2:14, 15b).

**Collect:** Water-thinned glue, paintbrushes, baby food jars, tissue paper in a variety of colors, wax paper, paper cups, scissors, and votive candles

## Here's What to Do:

Before class begins, make a mixture of half water and half glue.

Set the tissue paper in the middle of the room and instruct kids to cut the paper into small (no smaller than ½ inch) pieces. When each student has made a small pile of paper, distribute baby food jars, paintbrushes, and paper cups of water-thinned glue. Have students paint a small area on each jar with glue then cover the area with small pieces of tissue paper. Encourage each child to use a variety of colors as he or she works to cover the entire jar with two or three layers of paper. Show kids how to coat the finished jars with thinned glue.

Set the jars on a sheet of wax paper in a sunny spot to dry. Explain that kids can place small votive candles inside their jars and enjoy a colorful glow.

## For Further Fun:

● If some students want to make additional, larger candleholders, olive jars work well. Some students may want to use their candleholders to set up a worship center in your classroom or centers in their homes.

● When the candleholders have dried, students may use a black marker to print messages such as "Jesus is the light" or "Shine like stars" on them.

# 3. Shine On

*Students will make punched-tin candleholders.*

**Theme:** Loving words and actions are reflections of Jesus.

**Scripture Spotlight 1:** "A city that is built on a hill cannot be hidden. And people don't hide a light under a bowl. They put it on a lampstand so the light shines for all the people in the house" (Matthew 5:14b, 15).

**Scripture Spotlight 2:** "You will be my witnesses—in Jerusalem, in all of Judea, in Samaria, and in every part of the world" (Acts 1:8b).

**Collect:** Empty tin cans (soup cans or #2 fruit cans work well), newspapers, hammers, nails, paper, tape, pencils, and votive candles

## Here's What to Do:

A day or two before class, fill clean, empty tin cans with water. (You'll need one can for each student.) Place the cans in the freezer until the water is frozen solid.

When class begins, give each student a piece of paper that has been cut to fit around a tin can. Tell kids to each draw a simple design on the paper, such as a star, cross, dove, fish, or angel. Show them the sample designs in the margin.

Cover the work surface with stacks of newspapers. Give each child a hammer, a nail, and a frozen can. Show kids how to place the paper patterns around the cans and tape them in place. Then demonstrate how to use a hammer and a nail to make holes about ½ inch apart along the design lines.

After kids have completed their designs, run warm water over the cans so the ice blocks melt and fall out. Then have children dry their cans and place votive candles inside.

When students get home, they can light the candles with adult assistance. Caution children that the candleholders may get hot when lit candles are inside.

## For Further Fun:

● You may pair older children with younger students. Older students can help hold the cans or hammer the designs.

● Have kids light their candles in class. As kids light their candles, allow them to share ways they'd like to be lights to the world in the coming week.

# 4. Splatter Strings

*Kids will color super shoelaces they can wear.*

**Theme:** God is glorified when we do good things.

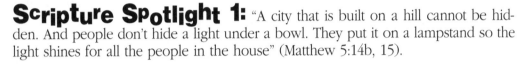

**Scripture Spotlight 1:** "You should be a light for other people. Live so that they will see the good things you do and will praise your Father in heaven" (Matthew 5:16b).

**Scripture Spotlight 2:** "If you eat or drink, or if you do anything, do it all for the glory of God" (1 Corinthians 10:31).

**Collect:** White shoelaces, water-soluble markers, spray bottles, and plastic garbage bags (optional: glitter paint)

# Here's What to Do:

Cover your work space with plastic garbage bags and scatter colorful water-soluble markers on the table. Give kids two white shoelaces apiece and tell them to randomly dot the laces with several markers of different colors. As children work, explain that Jesus called his followers to be lights to the world so that people will see a difference in us when we're following Jesus. Tell them that just as these fun shoelaces will stand out and be different, so their faith will make a difference in the way they live.

When they've finished, have kids place their colored shoelaces flat on the covered work surface. Show kids how to use the spray bottles to wet the laces. As the laces get wet, the colors will begin to spread and blend. Be sure kids don't drench the shoelaces, but be sure the laces are damp. Hang the laces to dry, being sure to protect the surface underneath the project from drips. Kids may want to add dots of glitter paint, even if the laces are damp. Instruct parents to put the laces in the dryer before children wear them.

# For Further Fun:

● Instead of lacing shoes with the colored laces, braid groups of three of them together to make Bible bookmark gifts.

● Girls may want to wear the laces in their hair as brightly colored bows.

# Sermon on the Mount (Part 2)

**T**hose who heard the Sermon on the Mount must have thought Jesus' words were radical and revolutionary. Jewish tradition had turned God's law into a complicated system of do's and don'ts. But Jesus turned the Law into a simple matter of love for God and love for others. Jesus' words are as powerful today as they were 2,000 years ago. The activities in this section can help kids realize that Jesus cares about their attitudes as well as their actions.

**1.** Being kind to enemies is no easy task. But Jesus clearly commands us to love and pray for our enemies (Matthew 5:44). Idea 1, "Prayer Pals," will allow children to create reminders of the miracles that can happen when they pray for their enemies.

**2.** Jesus encouraged his listeners to focus on heavenly, rather than earthly, things. That's difficult for adults and much more difficult for children! Jesus challenged his followers to store indestructible treasures in heaven rather than scramble to gather treasures here on earth (Matthew 6:19-21). Use Idea 2, "True Treasures," to help kids learn about the indestructible treasures God has for us.

**3.** God created everything in the world to live together in a delicate balance. Jesus urged his listeners to depend on God just as the flowers of the field and the birds of the air do (Matthew 6:25-29). Use Idea 3, "Beautiful Nature," to make reminders of God's beautiful world around us.

**4.** Jesus tells us that God is a loving Father who wants to give good gifts to his children. Jesus' words remind us that all we need to do is seek God and ask him for what we need (Matthew 7:7-8). Idea 4, "Door Decor," will remind children that God hears and cares—they only need to knock!

**5.** Jesus taught that the only way to achieve stability in our lives is to build on a strong foundation—faith in the living God (Matthew 7:24-27). People who build their lives on other foundations face certain disaster. Use Idea 5, "Sturdy Castles," to show kids that God holds our lives together.

# 1. Prayer Pals

*Kids will make prayer pals that will remind them to pray.*

**Theme:** Pray for friends and enemies.

**Scripture Spotlight 1:** "But I say to you, love your enemies. Pray for those who hurt you" (Matthew 5:44).

**Scripture Spotlight 2:** "Pray in the Spirit at all times with all kinds of prayers, asking for everything you need. To do this you must always be ready and never give up" (Ephesians 6:18).

**Collect:** Scraps of nylon hose, thread, sewing needles, markers, fiberfill or cotton balls, glue, scissors, poster board, and small pieces of magnetic strip

## Here's What to Do:

Before class, cut two 4-inch circles from the nylon hose and two 2-inch circles from the poster board for each student.

Give each child two circles of nylon hose, two 2-inch circles of poster board, a sewing needle, and a 12-inch length of thread. Show kids how to stitch around the edge of one circle of nylon, about ½ inch from the edge. Then demonstrate how to gently pull the thread taut so that it pulls the edges of the nylon together. Then have kids stuff pieces of fiberfill or cotton balls into their "nylon bags" until they're quite full. Show kids how to pull the thread, close the bags, then make a few more stitches to seal them.

Set out markers and have kids draw sad faces on the front of their pieces of nylon. When they've finished, have kids glue their Prayer Pals to their poster board circles. Then have them remove the backing from the magnetic pieces and stick them on the back of the poster-board circles.

Repeat the process with the other circles of nylon, but this time have kids draw happy faces. Explain that these Prayer Pals are reminders that when we pray for our enemies, we turn them into friends.

## For Further Fun:

● Kids may want to make their Prayer Pals more elaborate by stitching the eyes, noses, and mouths. They can make eyes and mouths by stitching from front to back several times in the same spots. They can create noses by using the same method used to make the heads: Stitch loosely in a circle, then gently pull the thread taut to form a "bag." Use the needles to push a small amount of fiberfill into the noses to make them puffy.

● Kids can use yarn and fabric scraps to create hair, clothes, or hats for their Prayer Pals.

# 2. True Treasures

*Help kids make jeweled treasure boxes.*

**Theme:** Our real treasures are in heaven.

**Scripture Spotlight 1:** "But store your treasures in heaven where they cannot be destroyed by moths or rust and where thieves cannot break in and steal them. Your heart will be where your treasure is" (Matthew 6:20-21).

**Scripture Spotlight 2:** "Respect for the Lord is the greatest treasure" (Isaiah 33:6b).

**Collect:** Colorful hard candies, gold spray paint, newspaper, glue, scissors, crayons, one margarine tub or oatmeal box for each child, and photocopies of the "Greatest Treasure" handout (p. 76)

## Here's What to Do:

Before class, make enough photocopies of the "Greatest Treasure" handout (p. 76) so each child has one copy.

Distribute margarine tubs or oatmeal boxes and have kids take them outside and lay them upside down on sheets of newspaper. Help kids spray paint the outside of their margarine tubs completely. Allow the tubs to dry thoroughly. While the tubs are drying, have kids cut out and color the verse from the "Greatest Treasure" handout.

When the tubs have dried, have kids retrieve them and set them on clean sheets of newspaper. Show kids how to glue the verse to their lids. Then give students each a handful of colored hard candies and have them glue the candy "jewels" around the Bible verse on the lid.

## For Further Fun:

● When the treasure boxes are dry, have kids write on slips of paper acts of kindness or service that they plan to do in the coming weeks. Have kids store these in their treasure boxes, draw one out each day, and try to do it. Explain that when we show others kindness and love, we're storing treasures in heaven.

# 3. Beautiful Nature

*Kids will create floral wreaths from paper sacks.*

**Theme:** God cares for the world around us.

**Scripture Spotlight 1:** "And why do you worry about clothes? Look at how the lilies in the field grow. They don't work or make clothes for themselves. But I tell you that even Solomon with his riches was not dressed as beautifully as one of these flowers" (Matthew 6:28-29).

**Scripture Spotlight 2:** "And God can give you more blessings than you need. Then you will always have plenty of everything—enough to give to every good work" (2 Corinthians 9:8).

**Collect:** Paper grocery sacks, 8-inch (or smaller) foam or straw wreaths, straight pins with colored or pearl heads, pinking shears, pencils, markers, and silk leaves or green tissue paper

## Here's What to Do:

Give each child an 8-inch wreath, a paper grocery sack, 10 straight pins, and pinking shears. If you're short on pinking shears, have kids form pairs and share them. Set out markers for children to share. Have students use the pinking shears to cut 10 1½-inch squares and 10 1-inch squares from the paper sacks. Instruct kids to fold each square on both diagonals to create an X on each square as shown in the margin. Then allow students a few moments to decorate their squares with markers if they wish.

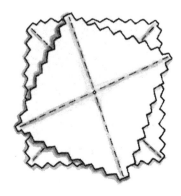

When kids have cut, creased, and colored their squares, show them how to lay a smaller paper square on top of each of the larger ones and then lay both squares on the wreath. Have children push a pin into the center of each "square pair," securing it to the wreath. Instruct kids to repeat this process with the rest of their paper squares until they've each created a wreath of paper flowers. When kids have finished attaching their flowers, show them how to fill gaps between the flowers by using the tips of pencils to push the ends of silk leaves or torn green tissue paper leaves into the wreaths.

# The Greatest Treasure

"But store your treasures in heaven... Your heart will be where your treasure is" (Matthew 6:20-21).

"But store your treasures in heaven... Your heart will be where your treasure is" (Matthew 6:20-21).

# For Further Fun:

● Instead of using paper sacks, use fabric scraps or old bluejeans to create flowers. Older kids or an adult helper can spray the fabric with starch and can iron creases into the fabric squares.

● Use a larger wreath and have kids work together to make a decoration for your classroom.

# 4. Door Decor

*Kids will make door decorations that jingle.*

**Theme:** God listens when we talk to him.

**Scripture Spotlight 1:** "Ask, and God will give to you. Search, and you will find. Knock, and the door will open for you" (Matthew 7:7).

**Scripture Spotlight 2:** "Here I am! I stand at the door and knock. If you hear my voice and open the door, I will come in and eat with you and you will eat with me" (Revelation 3:20).

**Collect:** Different colors of ribbon, scissors, glue, small pie tins (from pot pies), three jingle bells per student, nails, hammers, blocks of wood, markers, and photocopies of the "Ask, Search, and Knock" handout (p. 78)

# Here's What to Do:

Before class, make enough photocopies of the "Ask, Search, and Knock" handout (p. 78) for each child to have one.

Distribute small pie tins and have kids lay the tins upside down on blocks of wood. Then show kids how to use hammers and nails to make three holes at the bottom of the tins and two at the top, as shown in the margin. Allow kids to choose three lengths of ribbon apiece, each a different color, and cut each one to a different length. Have them poke the ribbons through the holes in the bottom of their tins then tie knots to keep the ribbons from slipping through. Next, instruct kids to tie a jingle bell to the end of each of their ribbons.

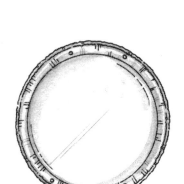

Distribute copies of the "Ask, Search, and Knock" handout and have kids color them and cut them out. Then have them glue the verses to the back of their pie tins. Allow each student to choose another color of ribbon, cut a 12-inch length of it, then poke each end of the ribbon through one of the holes at the top of the tin. Have students secure the ribbon with knots to create hangers.

Kids can hang the door decorations in their houses as reminders that God listens when they talk to him.

# For Further Fun:

● Have kids choose new verses that they'd like to learn and tape them to the pie tins, where they'll see them every day.

● A student can hang the pie tin on a different family member's door each day as a means of encouragement.

# 5. Sturdy Castles

*Help kids make a sand castle that is held together with glue.*

**Theme:** God is a firm foundation for us to build upon.

# Ask, Search, and Knock

Ask, and God will give to you. Search, and you will find. Knock, and the door will open for you.

Matthew 7:7

**Scripture Spotlight 1:** "Everyone who hears my words and obeys them is like a wise man who built his house on rock. It rained hard, the floods came, and the winds blew and hit that house. But it did not fall, because it was built on rock" (Matthew 7:24-25).

**Scripture Spotlight 2:** "God is our protection and our strength. He always helps in times of trouble. So we will not be afraid even if the earth shakes, or the mountains fall into the sea, even if the oceans roar and foam, or the mountains shake at the raging sea" (Psalm 46:1-3).

**Collect:** Sand, flour, water, sugar, a saucepan, a large bucket, measuring cups and spoons, small cups and cans, and sturdy cardboard

# Here's What to Do:

Before class, make a paste by mixing 1 cup of water with ⅓ cup of flour and 2 tablespoons of sugar. Cook the paste until it turns clear. Cool the paste to room temperature.

Choose a student to measure 6 cups of sand and pour it into a large bucket. Have another volunteer pour in all of the flour paste. Have kids mix the sand and the paste together with their hands. As kids work with the mixture, gradually mix in water until the sand is like clay.

Dump the sand mixture onto a large piece of cardboard. Help kids build a sand castle. Explain that this sand castle will be different from the house built on the sand in Matthew 7:24-25 because it will hold together. Children can mound the sand with their hands or pack it into small cups and cans, then dump out the molded forms. Once kids feel satisfied with their sand creation, allow it to dry and harden overnight.

# For Further Fun:

● After the castle is built, give each child a cupful of sand to make miniature sand castles or sand shapes. See how fragile their individual sand castles are compared to the solid one built with the special mixture. Compare a life built on Christ with one built on other things.

● Have older children create an elaborate sand castle by including a working drawbridge made with sticks and string and by cutting windows and other details into the castle with plastic knives. The castle can be painted when it's dry.

# Jesus Feeds the 5,000 and Walks on Water

**A**s the Jewish Passover Feast drew near, Jesus performed two miracles, one very public and the other within the close circle of his friends. When thousands gathered along the shores of Lake Galilee to hear Jesus teach, Jesus multiplied a boy's lunch and used it to feed the whole crowd (John 6:1-12). Later, when his disciples were caught in stormy waters, Jesus walked to them on the water, calmed the storm, and banished their fears (John 6:16-21). Use these crafts and activities to help kids realize that Jesus still performs miracles in our world today.

**1.** When Jesus fed the 5,000, it was almost time for the Passover Feast. As a reminder of the first Passover (Exodus 12:1-30), many Jews today hang mezuzas on their doorposts to remind themselves of God's presence. Use Idea 1, "Passover Mezuzas," to help kids discover God's presence in their lives today.

**2.** When Jesus broke the bread to feed the crowds, there was so much left over that the disciples gathered up the leftovers in 12 baskets! Kids can weave their own baskets in Idea 2, "Lovely Baskets."

**3.** When a sudden storm caught the disciples on the Lake of Galilee, they feared for their lives. Then Jesus came to them, calmed the storm, and guided them safely to shore. Idea 3, "Frosty Fingers," will allow kids to create a storm while they experience a little of the discomfort that the disciples might have felt.

**4.** Late in the evening, Jesus' disciples set sail for Capernaum. After they'd gone a considerable distance across Lake Galilee, a storm struck, tossing the disciples' boat around as if it were a toy. Use Idea 4, "A Clean Getaway," to show kids how scary it must have been in the boat that night.

**5.** During the storm, wind and rain pelted the boat as waves crashed dangerously over its bow. How the drenched and quaking disciples must have wished for Jesus to comfort them! By making "Swirling Stationery" in Idea 5, kids can imagine the swirling waters that Jesus was able to calm.

# 1. Passover Mezuzas

*Children will create reminders of God's love and protection.*

**Theme:** God protects and takes care of his children.

**Scripture Spotlight 1:** "Jesus went up on a hill and sat down there with his followers. It was almost the time for the Jewish Passover Feast" (John 6:3-4).

**Scripture Spotlight 2:** "Always remember these commands I give you today" (Deuteronomy 6:6).

**Collect:** Photocopies of the "Mezuza" handout (p. 82) and the "Passover Parchment" handout (p. 83), crayons, glitter glue, glue sticks, scissors, pencils, and markers

## Here's What to Do:

Before class, make enough photocopies of the "Mezuza" handout (p. 82) and the "Passover Parchment" handout (p. 83) for each student to have one of each.

Tell kids that many Jews today remember the Passover by placing mezuzas on the doorposts of their houses. Explain that a mezuza is a reminder of the way God takes care of us and of the importance of his words.

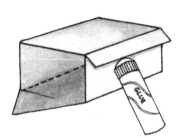

Give children "Mezuza" handouts and show them how to fold on the dotted lines and cut on the solid lines. Then allow them to decorate the back of the handouts with markers, crayons, or glitter glue. Have kids fold their papers into square "tubes" with their decorations on the outside. Direct each of them to glue flap A to the opposite side of the tube, as shown in the margin. Help them fold down the starred flaps and use glue sticks to glue them in place.

When kids have finished making their mezuzas, pass out the "Passover Parchment" handouts. Have kids cut the verses apart and roll them around pencils to create scrolls. Children can then place the scrolls inside their mezuzas.

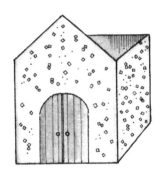

When students get home, they can tack the mezuzas to their door frames as reminders of God's love.

## For Further Fun:

● Make a mezuza for your classroom. Before you start class each week, choose a student to read one of the scrolls and pray, thanking God for his love and protection.

● Have kids write down other favorite verses on slips of paper, roll them up, and place them in the mezuza.

# 2. Lovely Baskets

*Kids will weave heart-shaped baskets to fill with goodies.*

**Theme:** God provides for our every need.

**Scripture Spotlight 1:** "So they gathered up the pieces and filled twelve baskets with the pieces left from the five barley loaves" (John 6:13).

**Scripture Spotlight 2:** "My God will use his wonderful riches in Christ Jesus to give you everything you need" (Philippians 4:19).

**Collect:** Photocopies of the "Lovely Baskets" handout (p. 85); ½×9-inch strips of colored paper; scissors; glue sticks; and treats such as nuts, berries, and raisins

# Mezuza

Front

# Passover Parchment

------------------------------------------------------------

"Know and believe today that the Lord is God. He is God in heaven above and on the earth below. There is no other god!" (Deuteronomy 4:39).

------------------------------------------------------------

"You must not use the name of the Lord your God thoughtlessly, because the Lord will punish anyone who uses his name in this way" (Deuteronomy 5:11).

------------------------------------------------------------

"Honor your father and your mother" (Deuteronomy 5:16a).

------------------------------------------------------------

"You must not steal" (Deuteronomy 5:19).

------------------------------------------------------------

"You must not tell lies about your neighbor" (Deuteronomy 5:20).

------------------------------------------------------------

"Love the Lord your God with all your heart, all your soul, and all your strength" (Deuteronomy 6:5).

------------------------------------------------------------

"Forget about the wrong things people do to you . . . Love your neighbor as you love yourself" (Leviticus 19:18a).

------------------------------------------------------------

### Here's What to Do:

Before class, make enough photocopies of the "Lovely Baskets" handout (p. 85) for each student to have two. If possible, photocopy them on colored paper.

Give students two handouts apiece and have them cut along the solid lines and fold on the dotted lines. Remind kids to fold *in* on the dotted lines so the lines won't show in the finished projects.

Begin with the top strip of the piece in your right hand and show students how to weave the basket by slipping the folded strip around and through the strips on the left side, rather than over and under. Do the opposite with the next strip, slipping it through where the other went around and around where the other went through. Although younger kids will get the hang of this once they start, you may want the older students to lend them a hand as they begin the process.

Allow students to choose ½×9-inch strips of colored paper. Kids can write Philippians 4:19 on the handles and glue the ends to the inside of the baskets. Provide treats such as nuts, berries, or raisins to fill the baskets. Then have kids give the baskets to friends, siblings, or parents.

### For Further Fun:

● Spread a sheet on the floor and have kids sit around it. After reading John 6:1-12, sprinkle small treats such as crackers or cookies on the sheet and have each child take a handful. When kids have finished their handfuls, have them collect the remainder of the treats in their baskets.

# 3. Frosty Fingers

*Kids will re-create the swirling waters of Lake Galilee—and feel them, too!*

### Theme: Jesus has the power to do anything.

### Scripture Spotlight 1: "When they had rowed the boat about three or four miles, they saw Jesus walking on the water, coming toward the boat" (John 6:19).

### Scripture Spotlight 2: "Then Jesus came to them and said, 'All power in heaven and on earth is given to me' " (Matthew 28:18).

### Collect: Several trays of ice, bowls, spoons, blue and green powdered tempera, newsprint, crayons, and markers

### Here's What to Do:

Form trios and give each trio a large sheet of newsprint, crayons, and several ice cubes in a bowl. Instruct kids to lay the papers widthwise. Be sure kids are working on a hard surface, rather than on carpet.

Explain that the bottom half of the papers are going to be Lake Galilee and that kids can use the crayons to create any fish, shells, or plant life that they wish. As groups finish, have a representative from each trio take a spoonful of the blue and green powdered tempera and sprinkle it over the lower half of the group's picture. When everyone is finished with the paint, allow groups to rub ice cubes over the paint. Remind kids that if they rub too much over one spot, the paper will become weak and will tear. Encourage kids to make waves, swirls, and splashes in their pictures.

Have kids place their papers in the sun or another warm spot where the pictures can dry while they clean their hands and throw away any unused ice. When the

# Lovely Baskets

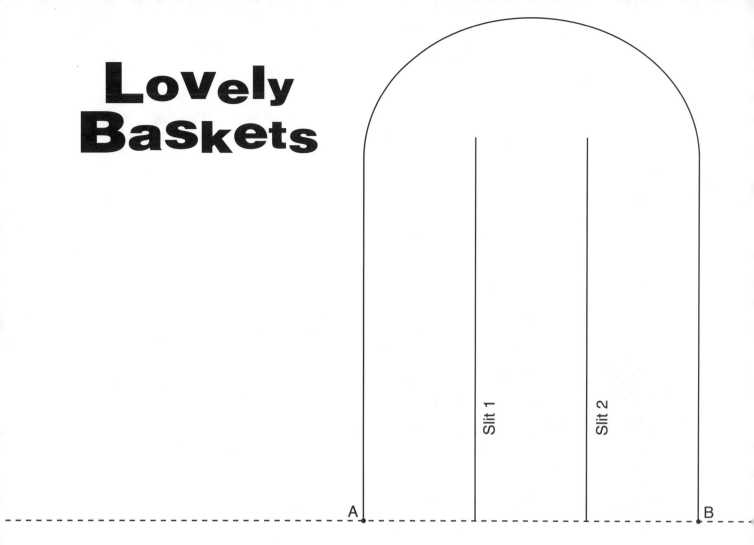

Slit 1

Slit 2

A

B

paint is nearly dry, have trios work together to draw small boats, Jesus, and storm clouds. When the pictures are finished, hang them around the room.

## For Further Fun:
● Turn the lights down and play storm sounds as kids work.
● When the paint dries thoroughly, sprinkle a little black paint on the upper half of each painting and have kids create swirling winds and dark storm clouds.
● Make your room into Lake Galilee by having kids ice-paint a wall-sized mural. Then have kids act out the story of the disciples in the storm.

# 4. A Clean Getaway

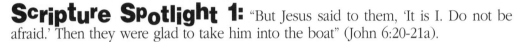

*Kids will make soap boats that float.*

### Theme: Jesus can calm our fears.

### Scripture Spotlight 1: "But Jesus said to them, 'It is I. Do not be afraid.' Then they were glad to take him into the boat" (John 6:20-21a).

### Scripture Spotlight 2: "God is our protection and our strength. He always helps in times of trouble" (Psalm 46:1).

### Collect: Soap powder (such as Ivory Snow), water, watercolor paints, a measuring cup, paintbrushes, wax paper, plastic spoons, paper triangles, toothpicks, and bowls

## Here's What to Do:
Have kids form pairs, and set out a bowl and plastic spoon for each pair. Place 1 cup of soap powder in each bowl and have one partner add 3 spoonfuls of water. Then have the other partner knead the mixture with his or her hands until it's smooth. Have partners divide their soap mixture in half so that they each have a small handful.

Show students how to roll the soap into an egg-shaped ball then work it into the shape of a boat. This is easily done if they press their thumbs in the center of the ball then work them out to the sides. Show kids how to make sails by poking toothpicks through paper triangles.

When students have finished sculpting their boats, have them set the sculptures on squares of wax paper. Provide watercolor paints and paintbrushes so kids can decorate the boats however they wish.

NOTE: Make sure kids know that these soap boats will disintegrate if they stay in water too long. Students wishing to keep their boats intact will need to keep them dry!

## For Further Fun:
● Bring a small inflatable wading pool and fill it with water. Have two or three students take part in a boat race by blowing their boat to the opposite side of the pool. Onlookers may make rough water by splashing gently.
● Before kids decorate their boats, have them poke a small hole in each bow then string a length of yarn through it. Then they can pull the boats to safety in "rough water."

# 5. Swirling Stationery

*Kids will design unique marbled paper.*

**Theme:** God is near when we call.

**Scripture Spotlight 1:** "They saw Jesus walking on the water, coming toward the boat. The followers were afraid, but Jesus said to them, 'It is I. Do not be afraid' " (John 6:19b).

**Scripture Spotlight 2:** "My help comes from the Lord, who made heaven and earth" (Psalm 121:2).

**Collect:** Liquid starch, acrylic paints, acrylic medium (or extender), paintbrushes, foam egg cartons, glass baking or casserole dishes, heavy card-stock note paper and envelopes, hair picks or toothpicks, measuring spoons, newsprint, paper towels, cups of water, and a sink

# Here's What to Do:

Before kids arrive, set up one marbling station for every three kids in your class. Spread newsprint on the floor at each station then pour liquid starch into each of the glass baking or casserole dishes (one at each station) so it's about 1 inch deep. Place about 1½ teaspoons of acrylic paint in each section of a foam egg carton. Add a few drops of acrylic medium to each color to thin it out. Then set one egg carton, paintbrushes, a hair pick or several toothpicks, a cup of water, note paper, and envelopes at each marbling station.

Form groups of no more than three and send each group to a marbling station. Explain that kids will be making paper that looks like the swirling waters that Jesus calmed. Lead kids through the following steps. Although only one child may marble at each station, others will enjoy watching the process.

1. Dip a paintbrush in one of the colors of paint and drip paint into the starch. Be sure to place drops at different places in the dish.

2. Repeat this process with two more colors, *thoroughly* rinsing the brush between colors.

3. Slowly drag a hair pick or a toothpick through the starch and paint to create a swirled design. Encourage children to try a variety of patterns.

4. Fold a piece of note paper in half and crease it firmly. Then slightly open the card and *carefully* lay the face of it on the starch and paint. Gently press the edges down so they touch the surface of the paint.

5. Remove the paper and walk to a sink. Under a light flow of water, rinse the starch from the surface of the card. Then lay the card flat on a sheet of newsprint to dry.

6. Repeat the process with the outer flap of an envelope.

Since trios will be using the same colors, there's no need to empty the starch between each use. However, if children want to trade colors with other trios, simply skim the starch with a paper towel or a sheet of newsprint. This will remove extra paint and "clean" the starch.

After the note cards and envelopes have dried, instruct kids to take them home and press them flat between several heavy books.

# For Further Fun:

● Kids can stack their note cards and envelopes, then tie them with ribbon. Add a few colorful pens for nice handmade gifts!

● Help children marble 1½-inch strips of heavy paper to make bookmarks. When the paint has dried, have kids punch a hole in the top of each bookmark and tie a ribbon through it.

# Parables on Growing

*Keep growing! That's God's message to Christians of all ages. Luke 8:15 says that those who listen to and obey God's Word will bear fruit for God's kingdom. Children need to see that when they obey God's Word, God will cause their faith to grow. Use the ideas in this section to help children grow in Christ.*

**1.** Just as small branches are attached to the main vine, we're attached to the source of all life—God. Once a flower or a vegetable is separated from the plant, it dies. In the same way, we must be firmly attached to God in order to grow and live productive lives. Use Idea 1, "Trained Branches," to illustrate how we can follow God and become more like him.

**2.** Plants don't grow properly if they receive too much sun, if they don't get enough water, or if the soil has too much clay or sand. Jesus said that those who hear the Word of God and obey it are like plants rooted in rich, fertile soil (Luke 8:15). Use Idea 2, "Planter Painters," to teach children that the right environment and the right nutrients make all the difference to plants and to Christians.

**3.** Jesus said that even if our faith is as small as a mustard seed, we can move mountains. He also said that the kingdom of heaven is like the tiny mustard seed that grows into a large plant. Clearly, we don't need to be completely grown up in Christ before we can start serving him. Even young Christians can make a difference. Use Idea 3, "Seeds of Faith," to help children see that with their faith in God they can do great things.

**4.** Christians never stop growing! Whether it's learning more about the Bible, strengthening our faith, discovering the power of prayer, or simply spending quiet times with God, spiritual growth takes time and effort. Use Idea 4, "Taller and Taller," to illustrate the need to mature in our faith.

**5.** It's hard to deny the goodness of fruit. Fruit that is sweet and juicy is the mark of a healthy tree. Christians are also called to bear fruit by leading others to Jesus, living out his commands, and growing in our relationship with him. Use Idea 5, "Sweet Fruit," to help children understand the importance of bearing fruit for God's kingdom.

# 1. Trained Branches

*Children will make topiary frames out of coat hangers.*

**Theme:** When we remain in God, we become like him.

**Scripture Spotlight 1:** "I am the vine, and you are the branches. If any remain in me and I remain in them, they produce much fruit. But without me they can do nothing" (John 15:5).

**Scripture Spotlight 2:** "Train yourself to serve God" (1 Timothy 4:7b).

**Collect:** Lightweight wire coat hangers, plastic containers such as large margarine bowls (with lids), pliers, potting soil, small rocks, small ivy plants, and scissors

## Here's What to Do:

Before this activity, have an adult volunteer help you cut one-third of the wire off each wire coat hanger. Then use pliers to twist the open end around the neck of the hanger.

Give each child one of these "shortened" wire hangers. Show kids how to bend the hooked end of each hanger so it's at a 90-degree angle to the rest of the hanger. Then have kids bend their hangers into simple shapes such as hearts, circles, and birds.

Have older children use scissors to poke a few holes into the bottom of the plastic containers. Instruct kids to place the container lids under the containers to act as saucers and to catch excess water. Help kids stand up their wire shapes in the containers and line the bottom of the containers with small rocks for drainage. Have children fill their containers with potting soil and plant the small ivy plants in the center of their pots, near the wire frames. Demonstrate how to gently wrap the vines around the frames. As the plants grow, children can continue wrapping them around the wire shapes until the wire is covered with ivy.

## For Further Fun:

● Have kids plant the topiary frames and the ivy plants in the clay pots from Idea 2.

● Have children name different leaves on the plants. They can give the leaves names of characteristics they want to grow in as Christians. Have them pray, touching each leaf, as they ask God to help them grow in those traits.

# 2. Planter Painters

*Help kids make painted pots for planting.*

**Theme:** Listen to and obey God so you may grow.

**Scripture Spotlight 1:** "And the seed that fell on the good ground is like those who hear God's teaching with good, honest hearts and obey it and patiently produce good fruit" (Luke 8:15).

**Scripture Spotlight 2:** "The earth causes plants to grow, and a garden causes the seeds planted in it to grow. In the same way the Lord God will make goodness and praise come from all the nations" (Isaiah 61:11).

**Collect:** Small clay flowerpots, a damp cloth, acrylic paints, paper plates, petroleum jelly, rags or small sponges, and a variety of leaves

## Here's What to Do:

Distribute the small clay flowerpots and have kids wipe them off with a damp cloth to remove any loose clay or dirt. Allow children to choose several leaves and decide how to place the leaves on their pots. Show children how to spread petroleum jelly on the leaves and press them (jelly side down) on their pots. The jelly will hold the leaves to the pots while the children paint around them.

Pour a small amount of acrylic paint onto each paper plate. Have kids dip rags or small sponges into the paint and dab it all over the pots. Kids may choose to mix colors, but the pots look very nice even if only one color is used. Tell kids not to put the paint on too thickly or the pots will take longer to dry. Also, they'll look nicer if some of the clay shows through.

When the paint has dried, have students carefully peel off the leaves.

## For Further Fun:

● Have kids fill their pots with potting soil and plant flower seeds such as marigolds, or herbs such as dill or mint. Place these in a sunny area of your classroom so kids can watch the growth process. Be sure to have someone water them!

● Allow kids to make additional pots that are opposite of their originals. Have them dab paint on leaves then press the painted leaves on pots.

# 3. Seeds of Faith

*Kids will create mosaics with seeds.*

**Theme:** Faith helps us accomplish great things.

**Scripture Spotlight 1:** "I tell you the truth, if your faith is as big as a mustard seed, you can say to this mountain, 'Move from here to there,' and it will move" (Matthew 17:20).

**Scripture Spotlight 2:** "The kingdom of God is like a mustard seed, the smallest seed you plant in the ground. But when planted, this seed grows and becomes the largest of all garden plants. It produces large branches, and the wild birds can make nests in its shade" (Mark 4:31-32).

**Collect:** A wide variety of seeds, beans, and uncooked rice; bowls; sturdy paper dessert plates; glue; scissors; photocopies of the "Mountain Movers" handout (p. 92); and black yarn

## Here's What to Do:

Before class, make enough photocopies of the "Mountain Movers" handout (p. 92) so each child may have one.

On a table set out a variety of seeds, beans, and uncooked rice (in separate bowls), glue, sturdy paper dessert plates, scissors, black yarn, and the "Mountain Movers" handouts. Have kids gather around the table so they have access to the different types of seeds. Distribute the handouts and have kids cut out the circles and glue them to the inside of their plates. Show kids how to outline the drawings by gluing the black yarn over the lines of the pictures. Be sure kids don't use too much glue, as it may cause the black dye to spread onto their fingers and the pictures.

After kids have outlined their pictures, explain that they'll use the seeds to fill in the drawings. Demonstrate that dried peas might be used for grassy areas, birdseed makes a nice sky, and sunflower seeds can make the mountains stand out. Encourage kids to be creative and to use seeds to fill in every area of their pictures.

## For Further Fun:

● Add variety to kids' choices by dyeing white rice blue for sky. Put the desired amount of rice in a sealable plastic bag with a teaspoon of food coloring and a tablespoon of rubbing alcohol. Squish the rice around with the food coloring and the alcohol until each piece is colored. Spread the rice on a newspaper to dry for several hours.

● As a finishing touch, kids can use the black yarn and whipstitch around the edge of the plates to make dark frames.

● Older students may choose to forego the handouts and create mountain pictures of their own.

# 4. Taller and Taller

*Kids will create cardboard people who grow taller.*

## Theme: Christians can grow every day.

## Scripture Spotlight 1: "Jesus became wiser and grew physically. People liked him, and he pleased God" (Luke 2:52).

## Scripture Spotlight 2: "But grow in the grace and knowledge of our Lord and Savior Jesus Christ. Glory be to him now and forever! Amen" (2 Peter 3:18).

## Collect: Cardboard (empty cereal boxes or poster board work well), paper fasteners, markers or paints, construction paper, glue, scissors, and rulers

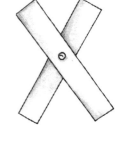

## Here's What to Do:

Before class, cut the cardboard into 1×8-inch strips. Each child will need six of these.

Distribute the cardboard strips. Show kids how to make an X with two of them by poking a hole at the intersection and fastening the two strips together with a paper fastener. Have them use the other four cardboard strips to make two more X's so each child has three X's.

Instruct each child to put one X in front of him or her then put a second X above it so the ends overlap. Have each one poke holes in the ends and attach the two X's with paper fasteners. Show them how to attach the third X in the same way. Then cut off the top two sections of the third X.

Have students cut feet, arms, and heads from construction paper, decorate them, and glue them to the cardboard frames as shown in the margin. When kids push the feet together, the cardboard people will grow taller. When they pull the feet apart, the cardboard people will shrink.

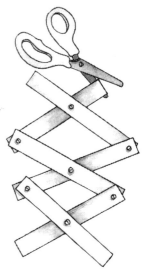

## For Further Fun:

● Have children tell about things that help them grow closer to Jesus, such as reading their Bibles, praying, or learning new things about God. Each time someone shares, have kids make their cardboard people grow a little.

● Using the cardboard figures, write and choreograph a puppet show for younger children. You can perform a familiar Bible story, or you can make up a contemporary story about growing in God.

# Mountain Movers

# 5. Sweet Fruit

*Kids will make fruit pizza together.*

**Theme:** Christians will bear fruit.

**Scripture Spotlight 1:** "And I give you this work: to go and produce fruit, fruit that will last" (John 15:16).

**Scripture Spotlight 2:** "But the Spirit produces the fruit of love, joy, peace, patience, kindness, goodness, faithfulness, gentleness, self-control. There is no law that says these things are wrong" (Galatians 5:22-23).

**Collect:** Prepared sugar-cookie dough, a baking sheet, a three-ounce package of cream cheese, powdered sugar, measuring cups and spoons, milk or water, assorted fresh fruit, apricot jam, lemon juice, a hot plate or a microwave, mixing bowls, a pastry brush, spoons, and knives

## Here's What to Do:

Before you begin, have kids wash their hands. Form four groups and explain that they'll all be helping to make a fruity snack to celebrate the fruit of the Spirit. Set up group 1 first then, while they're working, set up the other groups.

Have group 1 pat the prepared sugar-cookie dough into a big circle on the baking sheet. Bake the big cookie according to the directions on the package, being careful not to let it burn. (Group 1 can also help later with cleanup.)

Help group 2 mix the cream cheese with a cup of powdered sugar and about a teaspoon of milk or water until the mixture is spreadable. When the cookie has baked and cooled, allow group 2 to spread the cream cheese frosting on it.

While the other groups are working, have group 3 cut the fresh fruit into bite-sized pieces and mix the fruit with a couple teaspoons of lemon juice. Good fruit choices are seedless grapes, strawberries, kiwi, oranges, bananas, and apples—any fruit with edible seed will work great. After group 2 has spread the frosting on the cookie, group 3 may arrange the fruit on top of the frosting.

Have group 4 mix ½ cup of apricot jam with one tablespoon of water. They may heat the mixture on a hot plate or in a microwave until it's thin. Have students brush or drizzle the apricot glaze over the fruit. Cut the fruit pizza into wedges and enjoy it.

## For Further Fun:

● Make a few smaller crusts ahead of time. Then form trios and have each trio work on its own pizza. Kids can sample squares of each other's pizza to see what unique combinations they used.

● Kids can make bite-sized pizzas by using small, flat sugar cookies as their crusts.

# The Lost Sheep

*J*esus loved children. He talked about their value, their humility, and the example they set for adults with their willingness to trust. Jesus' parable about the lost sheep sends a message to adults: Watch after these precious treasures—they're important! Use the ideas in this section to help kids discover how much Jesus loves and values them.

**1.** When the disciples fought over who was the greatest in the kingdom of heaven, Jesus called a child forward. He wanted others to realize the importance of children and of being childlike (Matthew 18:10). Kids will feel important when they see themselves as the center of attention in Idea 1, "Framed."

**2.** Just as shepherds keep their ever-watchful eyes on their flocks (John 10:2-5), your kids will want to keep a close watch on this tasty flock! Use Idea 2, "Sheep Treats," to allow kids to make unique, edible sheep!

**3.** This passage tells kids how important each individual is to God (Matthew 18:12). God wants us to spread this message of his love and care to others. In Idea 3, "Ninety-Nine Plus One," kids can make necklaces to share that message with others.

**4.** Matthew 18:14 tells us that the heavenly Father wants to bring everyone to him. Idea 4, "Lamb Puppets," will give kids a chance to make friends they can keep close at hand, too.

# 1. Framed

*Kids will make drapery-ring picture frames that will put them in the spotlight.*

**Theme:** Jesus loves children.

**Scripture Spotlight 1:** "In the same way, your Father in heaven does not want any of these little children to be lost" (Matthew 18:14).

**Scripture Spotlight 2:** "But Jesus said, 'Let the little children come to me. Don't stop them, because the kingdom of heaven belongs to people who are like these children' " (Matthew 19:14).

**Collect:** Wooden drapery rings or colorful shower-curtain rings, empty cereal boxes or poster board, ribbon, craft "jewels" or ribbon roses, glitter, glue, a glue gun, pencils, scissors, and an instant-print camera or a 1×2-inch school picture of each child

## Here's What to Do:

Before class, use the instant-print camera to photograph children who didn't bring school pictures. Take the photos at a distance so the trimmed pictures will fit inside the drapery or shower-curtain rings.

Give each child a drapery ring or a shower-curtain ring and a 4-inch square of cardboard or poster board. Show kids how to lay the rings on the cardboard and trace around the outer edge of the rings. Have students cut out their circles then carefully glue their pictures on the circles, making sure their faces are in the center.

Set out glitter and other decorating items and allow a few minutes for kids to decorate their drapery rings. When kids finish, show them how to make ribbon loops and glue them to the top of the cardboard circles. Then have them glue the drapery rings to the cardboard circles so the rings frame their pictures. Allow the picture frames to dry thoroughly before kids take them home.

## For Further Fun:

● Instead of the ribbon loops, kids can glue craft magnets to the back of their pictures. Then they can display their pictures on their refrigerators where all will see them.

● Make this a family craft by having family members bring in pictures of themselves. Have each family member make a drapery-ring frame, then glue them all to a length of ribbon. Place a hanging hook or bow at the top as a hanger.

# 2. Sheep Treats

*Kids will experience shepherding made easy—and delicious!*

**Theme:** We are all unique and special.

**Scripture Spotlight 1:** "Be careful. Don't think these little children are worth nothing" (Matthew 18:10a).

**Scripture Spotlight 2:** "Together you are the body of Christ, and each one of you is a part of that body" (1 Corinthians 12:27).

**Collect:** Angel food cake, white frosting, flaked coconut, pretzel sticks, green food coloring, a large cookie sheet, plastic knives, and sealable plastic bags

## Here's What to Do:

Give each child a square of angel food cake and a plastic knife. Instruct each one to sculpt a lamb from his or her square of cake then frost it and roll it in the flaked coconut. Give each student four pretzel sticks to use as legs. Show kids how to insert the pretzel sticks into the bodies.

Form pairs and give each pair a sealable plastic bag filled with coconut flakes. Have partners put two drops of green food coloring into their bag, seal it, then work together to squeeze the coconut around with the food coloring. When the coconut turns green, have kids pour it out onto a large cookie sheet to make a pasture.

Have children place their lambs on the pasture. See if children can pick out their own lambs from the herd by recognizing special markings and traits. Allow kids to show off their lambs before they eat them!

## For Further Fun:

● Provide other edible decorations such as sprinkles, colored sugar, and jimmies to help kids create unique sheep.

● As soon as you've positioned all the lambs in the green coconut pasture, take a photograph of it. Show the photo the following week and see how many children still recognize their own lambs (the true test of a good angel food cake shepherd).

# 3. Ninety-Nine Plus One

*Kids will make their own lost-lamb necklaces.*

**Theme:** We were all found by God.

**Scripture Spotlight 1:** "If a man has a hundred sheep but one of the sheep gets lost, he will leave the other ninety-nine on the hill and go to look for the lost sheep" (Matthew 18:12).

**Scripture Spotlight 2:** "God loved the world so much that he gave his one and only Son so that whoever believes in him may not be lost, but have eternal life" (John 3:16).

**Collect:** 20 inches of leather lacing per child, a microwave or conventional oven, craft clay (recipe below), toothpicks, markers, acrylic paints, and paintbrushes

## Here's What to Do:

Give each child a piece of craft clay about the size of your thumb. Have each one mold the clay into a teardrop shape then use a toothpick to carve the shape of a lamb. Explain that this represents the lost sheep in the story. Have each child make a hole above the lamb, large enough for the leather lacing to slide through.

When children have finished, microwave the pendants on medium power for 10 to 12 minutes or bake them in a 350-degree oven for 15 minutes. If the pendants aren't quite dry yet, heat them for an additional 5 minutes.

Allow the baked pendants to cool for a few minutes. Then give children time to paint and decorate their lambs. Help children thread the lost-lamb pendants onto their leather lacing, then tie the lacing in a sturdy knot.

**Recipe for Craft Clay**
2 cups baking soda
1 cup cornstarch
1¼ cups cold water

Stir together baking soda and cornstarch in saucepan. Add water and cook over medium heat, stirring constantly. When the mixture becomes thick, turn it onto a plate and cover it until it's cool enough to handle. Knead gently and store in an air-tight container.

## For Further Fun:

● Have kids make a few extra clay lambs. Play a game of Hide-and-Seek: Have kids take turns hiding their lambs around the room for other students to find.

# 4. Lamb Puppets

*Kids will make special friends to keep close at hand.*

**Theme:** God values us and wants us to stay close to him.

**Scripture Spotlight 1:** "In the same way, your Father in heaven does not want any of these little children to be lost" (Matthew 18:14).

**Scripture Spotlight 2:** "But I am close to God, and that is good. The Lord God is my protection" (Psalm 73:28a).

**Collect:** An old black or white sock for each child, ½-inch black pompons or wiggly eyes, pencils, black or white felt, red felt, glue or a hot-glue gun, scissors, a black marker, and cotton balls (optional: ribbon and one jingle bell for each child)

## Here's What to Do:

Give each child one black or white sock, two ½-inch pompons or wiggly eyes, two 3×2-inch pieces of black or white felt to match the sock, and one 1×2-inch piece of red felt. Show kids how to put the socks on their hands then press some of the cloth between their fingers and thumbs to make puppets. Have kids use the pencils to make dots where they think the sheep's eyes should go, then glue the pompons over the pencil marks. Show kids how to trim the edges from all of the felt pieces so that one end on each is rounded. Using the felt that matches the socks, have kids pinch the square ends and glue them to the heads where ears would go. Then have each student glue a red piece of felt—the tongue—inside the lamb's mouth. Although white glue dries in about a minute, you may want to use a hot-glue gun to speed up drying time.

Give each of the children a handful of cotton balls (at least 10) and have them glue the cotton balls to the top of their puppets' heads. If students are making black sheep, they can color the cotton balls with a marker before gluing them.

Option: Give each child 4 to 5 inches of ribbon. Have each one slip a jingle bell on the ribbon then tie the ribbon around the sheep's neck.

## For Further Fun:

● Have kids put their puppets on their hands then place their hands behind their backs. Choose one child to be the shepherd and have the shepherd close his or her eyes. Select one child to hide his or her puppet somewhere in the room, then call the shepherd. See if the shepherd can discover whose sheep is "lost" then find the lost sheep.

● Groups of four can work together to put on a sock-puppet show. They may tell the story of the lost sheep or create a new story to perform.

# The Prodigal Son

**A** *foolish son turns away from his father, squanders his inheritance, and soon finds himself hungry and alone. When the son makes his way back home, hoping to rejoin his family as a servant, the father joyfully welcomes him and prepares a feast in his honor (Luke 15:11-24). Jesus told this parable in response to the Pharisees' criticism that Jesus accepted sinners and ate with them (Luke 15:1-2). The parable might well be titled "The Forgiving Father," for it focuses on the father's unconditional love for the wayward son. Use the activities in this section to bring the story of the prodigal son to life and to help your students realize that our loving God will always welcome them with open arms.*

**1.** At his lowest point, the son longed to fill his own stomach with the husks he was feeding to pigs. In the midst of his hunger and depression, the son realized that he could return to his father and ask for a position as a servant (Luke 15:16-17). Use Idea 1, "Just Say 'Oink,' " to remind kids that they can turn to God at any time in their lives.

**2.** The son must have been filthy from his impoverished situation and the long journey home. Despite the boy's disheveled state, the father ordered that the best robe be brought to him (Luke 15:22). When we come to God stained with sin, God makes us clean and gives us his very best. Use Idea 2, "Regal Robes," to make reminders of the new things we put on when God forgives us.

**3.** In Bible times, a signet was a symbol of power. When the father gave his son a signet ring, he was actually giving the son the authority to act on the father's behalf. Idea 3, "Simple Signets," will help kids realize that they're important to God.

**4.** The party the father threw for his son was quite a celebration: feasting, music, and dancing in honor of a lost son who had returned home (Luke 15:23-25). Idea 4, "Party Poppers," will show kids that God celebrates when they come back to him.

**5.** The prodigal son came back to a loving and forgiving father. We too can come back to God the Father when we've sinned. With Idea 5, "The Comeback Kid," help children realize that God's loving arms are always open.

# 1. Just Say "Oink"

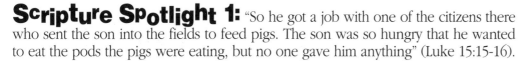

*Children will recycle those milk bottles to create piggy banks.*

**Theme:** God is with us, even in difficult times.

**Scripture Spotlight 1:** "So he got a job with one of the citizens there who sent the son into the fields to feed pigs. The son was so hungry that he wanted to eat the pods the pigs were eating, but no one gave him anything" (Luke 15:15-16).

**Scripture Spotlight 2:** "Even if I walk through a very dark valley, I will not be afraid, because you are with me" (Psalm 23:4a).

**Collect:** Clean, empty plastic one-gallon milk containers (with lids); glue; scissors; pencils; colored felt; corks; and pink or black chenille wire (optional: hot-glue gun)

## Here's What to Do:

Give each student a clean, empty plastic one-gallon milk container. Set the rest of the materials in the middle of the table where everyone has access to them. Explain that kids will be making piggy banks from the containers. Have kids turn each container on its side so the handle is on top. Show them how to glue four corks on the bottom to represent legs. For extra support and faster drying, you may want to use a hot-glue gun.

Have students cut eyes from the colored felt and glue them just under the handles. Help kids cut ears from the felt and glue them on either side of the eyes. Then allow students to cut circles to glue all over their pigs' bodies to look like spots. When students are satisfied with their pigs, help them each poke a small hole in the back and slip a piece of pink or black chenille wire into it. Kids can twist the wire tails around pencils to make them curly. Then help students cut slits in the pigs' backs to put their coins in. They can shake the money out through the "noses" or spouts.

## For Further Fun:

● Make a piggy bank for your class and set up a fund for a local charity. When your bank is full, have kids count the money and choose what organization it should be given to.

● Kids can choose to make dogs, cows, or other animals from their milk cartons.

# 2. Regal Robes

*Kids will create robes from oversized T-shirts.*

**Theme:** God covers us with his very best.

**Scripture Spotlight 1:** "But the father said to his servants, 'Hurry! Bring the best clothes and put them on him' " (Luke 15:22a).

**Scripture Spotlight 2:** "Look, I have taken away your sin from you, and I am giving you beautiful, fine clothes" (Zechariah 3:4b).

**Collect:** A large T-shirt for each child, markers, yardsticks, fabric glue, sewing shears, scissors, pencils, newsprint, fabric paints, and assorted craft "jewels"

### Here's What to Do:

Give each student a large T-shirt. Instruct students to trace the outlines of their shirts onto newsprint then cut out the outlines. Set the cutouts aside for later use.

Form pairs and have one partner hold a yardstick steady while the other partner uses a pencil to draw a line down the front of his or her shirt. When both partners have drawn their lines, show kids how to use sewing shears to cut the front of the shirts along the lines. Have one partner in each pair draw a line of fabric glue down the inside of each open side of his or her shirt, then have the other partner roll the fabric to the inside to make a finished front.

Place the newsprint cutouts inside the shirts then show students how to attach plastic craft jewels around the collars of their robes, using dots of fabric glue. Allow kids to use the fabric paints to add designs to their robes.

### For Further Fun:

● Allow children to decorate each other's shirts with their best work. Be sure each child puts a design on every other child's robe so each robe represents the entire class.

● Provide brightly colored T-shirts rather than white ones. Cut holes in large garbage bags to make plastic aprons for the children, then spread more garbage bags over your work surface. Allow kids to use an eyedropper to carefully put drops of chlorine bleach on the shirts. Tell them that God takes our sins away just as bleach takes the color away from the shirts.

# 3. Simple Signets

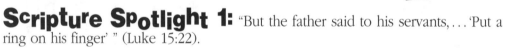

*Kids will make unique rings from plastic modeling clay.*

### Theme: We're important to God.

### Scripture Spotlight 1: "But the father said to his servants, . . . 'Put a ring on his finger' " (Luke 15:22).

### Scripture Spotlight 2: " 'I will make you important like my signet ring, because I have chosen you!' says the Lord All-Powerful" (Haggai 2:23b).

### Collect: Modeling compound (such as Fimo), paper clips, gold spray paint, and cookie sheets

### Here's What to Do:

Form pairs and give each pair six small balls of the modeling compound. Have kids roll the balls into thin ropes about the size of licorice strings. Instruct each partner to braid three strands together (younger children can twist two together). Have each partner fit the braided piece around the other partner's middle finger then press the ends together in front and pinch off any extra. Tell kids to carefully slide the rings off their partners' fingers and set the rings aside. Have pairs collect all of their leftover pieces into a ball then roll it out flat.

Show kids how to pinch off a piece of modeling compound approximately the size of a fingertip. Demonstrate how to flatten the compound, then use the end of an unbent paper clip to draw a simple design on it. When kids have each drawn a design in their compound, help them carefully push their designs onto their rings at the joints. It's helpful to score the back of the designs to help them adhere to the rings. Place the rings on cookie sheets and bake them according to package directions.

When the rings are dried and cool, take them outside and supervise as children spray them with gold spray paint. Students may wear their rings when they're completely dry.

## For Further Fun:

● Kids can create their own stationery by dripping wax from a candle onto the corner of a sheet of paper then pressing the designs from their signet rings into the wax as it begins to cool.

● Use a strip of felt to design a class banner. Drip candle wax onto the felt and allow kids to press their ring designs into the cooling wax.

# 4. Party Poppers

*Kids will make cardboard tubes for a great celebration!*

**Theme:** God celebrates when we follow him.

**Scripture Spotlight 1:** " 'My son was dead, but now he is alive again! He was lost, but now he is found!' So they began to celebrate" (Luke 15:24).

**Scripture Spotlight 2:** "In the same way, there is joy in the presence of the angels of God when one sinner changes his heart and life" (Luke 15:10).

**Collect:** Cardboard tubes (from toilet paper or paper towel rolls), scissors, 9-inch squares of colorful crepe paper or tissue paper, transparent tape, curling ribbon, and candy

## Here's What to Do:

If you're using tubes from paper towel rolls, cut them in half before class. Give each child at least one cardboard tube. Have each student choose his or her favorite color of crepe paper or tissue paper and set the tube in the center of the paper. Show kids how to roll the crepe paper around the tube then secure it with a piece of transparent tape. Have kids use curling ribbon to tie off one end of the paper, leaving a "tail." Help kids fill the tubes with candy, putting it through the open end, then tie off the end just like the other. Kids can use the scissors to fringe the ends and curl the ribbon.

## For Further Fun:

● Provide stickers or stamps for kids to use to decorate their poppers.

● Allow each student to make several poppers. Use these as prizes or party favors at a party planned by your students. Kids can think of games, songs, and snacks to make the celebration festive.

# 5. The Comeback Kid

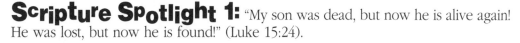

*Kids will make toys that will come back to them.*

**Theme:** We can come back to God, even when we sin.

**Scripture Spotlight 1:** "My son was dead, but now he is alive again! He was lost, but now he is found!" (Luke 15:24).

**Scripture Spotlight 2:** "There is joy in the presence of the angels of God when one sinner changes his heart and life" (Luke 15:10).

**Collect:** Tin cans with one end opened, a file, a hot-glue gun, jingle bells, 8- to 10-inch lengths of elastic string, nails, hammers, and tape

## Here's What to Do:

Before class, carefully file away any rough edges on the tin cans. You also may want to place thin lines of hot glue over the rough edges to make them smooth.

Give each child a can and place the other materials in the center of the table. Have kids use hammers and nails to poke a small hole in the center of the unopened end of each can. Then show kids how to tie the jingle bells onto one end of the 8- to 10-inch lengths of elastic string and tie the other end through the holes in the cans. If kids have made their holes too large, help them secure the elastic with hot glue or tape. When the cans are held with the open end up, the jingle bells should dangle below them (see diagram in margin).

As kids try to toss the jingle bells up and into the open end of the cans, remind them that the prodigal son was welcomed home with open arms.

## For Further Fun:

● Kids can make these toys with many different materials—paper cups, plastic tubs, small boxes, nuts and bolts, foil balls, or pompons.

● Have kids experiment with different lengths of elastic string.

# Jesus' Death and Resurrection

The ultimate tragedy became the ultimate victory. Jesus accepted death on the cross so he could offer us forgiveness and an eternally bright future in heaven. Jesus paid a terrible price, but we reap the rewards. Because of God's incomprehensible love and mercy, we can stand whole and blameless before our Maker. No wonder we joyfully shout, "He is risen! He is risen indeed." Use these ideas to help children see why Easter is a day for rejoicing.

**1.** Jesus' death on the cross made a bridge to God, crossing the yawning chasm of our sin and imperfection. It's hard to imagine how it felt to carry the sins of the world. Use Idea 1, "Forgiven," to help kids see that Jesus carried our sins to the cross so that we can be forgiven.

**2.** Jesus' resurrection means that we too can conquer death. Because Jesus is alive, we can have pure joy, we can live with God forever, we can enjoy life as forgiven people, and we can grow to become more like God. Use Idea 2, "Butterflies of Joy," to make tributes to all the gifts the Resurrection brings to us.

**3.** When Jesus died, the curtain that separated the Holy of Holies from the rest of the temple split in half (Matthew 27:51). This showed that because of Jesus' sacrifice, we can boldly approach God. Idea 3, "Knot to Worry," will help kids see that Jesus' sacrifice ties us closer to our Lord.

**4.** When the women went to the tomb on Sunday morning, they were horrified to see that the tomb was empty. When the angels said, "He is not here. He has risen from the dead as he said he would" (Matthew 28:6a), it was almost too much to believe. But Jesus did rise from the dead. Hundreds of people saw him. Use Idea 4, "Joy," to celebrate the joy and promise of the empty tomb.

**5.** Before Jesus ascended to heaven, he commanded his followers to go into all the world and make disciples. God has given each of us special gifts, abilities, and talents that make us uniquely outfitted to carry out that command. Use Idea 5, "Egg-stra Specially Made," to teach children what is special about each of them.

# 1. Forgiven

*Kids will make crosses of nails to remind them of Christ's sacrifice.*

**Theme:** Jesus carried our sins to the cross so we could be forgiven.

**Scripture Spotlight 1:** "Then they led him away to be crucified" (Matthew 27:31b).

**Scripture Spotlight 2:** "And through Christ, God has brought all things back to himself again—things on earth and things in heaven. God made peace through the blood of Christ's death on the cross" (Colossians 1:20).

**Collect:** Two 4-inch nails per child, thin-gauge wire, and leather lacing

## Here's What to Do:

Give each student two 4-inch nails and show everyone how to lay them in the shape of a cross then wrap the thin-guage wire around the place where the nails intersect. Be sure kids tuck in the ends of the wire so they won't scratch themselves. When kids have wrapped the nails securely, show them each how to slip a piece of leather lacing around the nails. Have kids tie the lacing loosely around their necks and wear the cross necklaces.

## For Further Fun:

● Have students take turns wearing all of the cross necklaces at once as an example of the weight of sin. Ask them how it feels to have all of the crosses removed at once.

# 2. Butterflies of Joy

*Kids will create colorful butterflies to celebrate the Resurrection.*

**Theme:** Jesus' resurrection brings us joy and life.

**Scripture Spotlight 1:** "Go quickly and tell his followers, 'Jesus has risen from the dead' " (Matthew 28:7a).

**Scripture Spotlight 2:** "Praise be to the God and Father of our Lord Jesus Christ. In God's great mercy he has caused us to be born again into a living hope, because Jesus Christ rose from the dead. Now we hope for the blessings God has for his children" (1 Peter 1:3-4a).

**Collect:** Coffee filters, water, newspaper, wax paper, black chenille wire, eyedroppers or drinking straws, food coloring, and old margarine tubs

## Here's What to Do:

Spread a thick layer of newspaper on the floor or outside. Fill each old margarine tub with water and several drops of red, yellow, or blue food coloring. Be sure you have at least two tubs of each color. Place two eyedroppers or drinking straws in each tub.

Give each student two coffee filters. Show kids how to drip colored water onto the filters to create designs and blend colors. Allow kids to color their filters however they wish, then place the filters on a sheet of wax paper in a warm, sunny place.

When the filters have dried, distribute two 5-inch lengths of black chenille wire to each student. Show kids how to pinch each filter together, wrap the wire around the middle, then bend the wire to make antennae. Have kids repeat the process with the other filters so they each have two butterflies. Hang the butterflies from your ceiling as reminders that Jesus' death and resurrection set us free.

## For Further Fun:

● Have each child create a banner, using a 12×24-inch rectangle of paper. Kids can write messages such as "Jesus lives" or "He is risen" on their banners, then tape one butterfly to each edge.

● Children can cut smaller circles from the coffee filters to make smaller butterflies.

# 3. Knot to Worry

*Kids will make paper knots with promises of God's love inside.*

**Theme:** Because of the Resurrection, we can boldy approach God.

**Scripture Spotlight 1:** "Then the curtain in the Temple was torn into two pieces, from the top to the bottom" (Matthew 27:51a).

**Scripture Spotlight 2:** "So, brothers and sisters, we are completely free to enter the Most Holy Place without fear because of the blood of Jesus' death" (Hebrews 10:19).

**Collect:** Shiny gift wrap, scissors, and markers

## Here's What to Do:

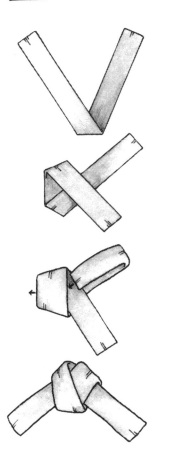

Before class, cut the shiny gift wrap into 18×4-inch sections. You'll need one of these for each student. Instruct students to write the words of John 3:16 on the plain side of the paper, then have them fold their sections in half lengthwise so the shiny paper shows on both sides. Demonstrate how to fold the strips of paper in the middle so they form V shapes. Then have each child fold the left side down, pointing to the right and crossing *over* the right side, as shown in the margin. Repeat this with the right side of the paper, and slip it through the hole made by the left side of the paper. Have each student pull both strips gently until they form a knot in the middle. Instruct kids to crease the knots so they lie flat.

## For Further Fun:

● Students can write the names of their family members and friends on the paper, then tie knots to symbolize their security in Jesus.

● Tape the paper knots on your wall, forming the shape of a heart.

# 4. Joy

*Kids will make eggs to show that the empty tomb fills us with joy.*

**Theme:** Rejoice! Jesus is alive!

**Scripture Spotlight 1:** "He is not here. He has risen from the dead as he said he would. Come and see the place where his body was" (Matthew 28:6).

**Scripture Spotlight 2:** "I am the One who lives; I was dead, but look, I am alive forever and ever!" (Revelation 1:18).

**Collect:** Balloons, tissue paper, a mixture of half glue and half water, pins, paintbrushes, and wax paper

## Here's What to Do:

Have each child blow up a balloon so it's approximately egg-shaped. Then show children how to tear off pieces of tissue paper, place them on the balloons, and "paint" over them with water-thinned glue. Have kids continue covering their balloons until they are entirely covered with tissue paper. Be sure that kids use plenty of glue and that the corners of the pieces of tissue paper are pressed down flat. When kids have covered their balloons, have them place the balloons on squares of wax paper and set them in a warm place to dry.

After the tissue paper has dried completely, allow kids to poke pins into the top part of the balloons to pop them. When the balloons pop, the tissue shells become very fragile, so warn kids to handle them with care. Show kids how the empty shells represent the empty tomb.

## For Further Fun:

● Have kids fill the shells with confetti then toss them at the ceiling. This may be messy, but kids will enjoy celebrating in such a fun fashion!

● Provide small candies, nuts, or raisins for kids to fill their eggs with. Allow students to deliver the eggs to a class of younger children.

# 5. Egg-Stra Specially Made

*Kids will make eggs with unique style.*

**Theme:** God gives each person special gifts, abilities, and talents.

**Scripture Spotlight 1:** "So go and make followers of all people in the world. Baptize them in the name of the Father and the Son and the Holy Spirit. Teach them to obey everything that I have taught you" (Matthew 28:19-20a).

**Scripture Spotlight 2:** "Something from the Spirit can be seen in each person, for the common good" (1 Corinthians 12:7).

**Collect:** Plastic-foam craft eggs; small pieces of scrap fabric, such as felt and denim, in solid colors; decorative trim; buttons; tacks or sewing pins; ribbon; butter knives; and paint pens

## Here's What to Do:

Set out the scrap fabric and give each student a plastic-foam egg. Have each child lay a piece of fabric on his or her egg then use a butter knife to push all of the fabric edges about a quarter of an inch into the plastic foam. The fabric edges should be embedded in the egg. Show kids how to line up another piece of fabric along one of the edges of the first piece of fabric. Show kids how to use the knife to push the edge of the second piece of fabric into the same slit that the first fabric is in. Then continue pushing in all edges of the second piece of fabric so that it's embedded in the plastic foam.

Instruct kids to continue until their eggs are covered with fabric pieces. They can also push in pieces of lace, ribbon, or other decorative trim. Buttons can be pushed in with tacks or sewing pins. Let each child decorate his or her egg in any pattern or design. Then have kids use paint pens to write their names and interests on the fabric patches.

# For Further Fun:

● Have an Easter egg hunt before the children write their names on the eggs. Have each child find an egg. When a child finds an egg made by someone else, have him or her try to guess who the egg belongs to.

● Instead of writing their own interests on the eggs, have children pass their eggs around and allow others to write affirmations on them.

# Paul's Travels

*Paul lived a fruitful life full of action and adventure. Acts 12–28 tells how Paul's newfound faith in Jesus led him to share the good news of God's grace, mercy, and love throughout the Mediterranean region. With God's help, Paul preached the gospel despite imprisonment, riots, plots against his life, shipwrecks, and snakebites. The ideas in this section will help kids realize that God will be with them as they share about his love.*

**1.** During his second missionary journey, Paul and his friends visited the Roman colony of Philippi. There they met a woman named Lydia, a seller of purple cloth, who invited Paul and his companions to her home. After listening to Paul's words, Lydia and all in her house were baptized and believed in Jesus (Acts 16:14-15). Idea 1, "The Color Purple," will help kids see that God chooses people from all walks of life to follow him.

**2.** Paul met all kinds of people during his travels. Two who became his good friends were Aquila and Priscilla, tent makers from Italy. Paul worked with them while he was in Corinth telling others about God's love. Idea 2, "Under the Big Top," will help children realize that they can use their talents to draw others to God, too.

**3.** Paul certainly lived out Jesus' command to tell others about God's love! His travels took him all over the Mediterranean and Europe, where he touched the lives of countless people. Idea 3, "Mapping out Adventure," will help kids remember that they need to tell others about Jesus, too.

**4.** Between A.D. 59 and 60, Paul sailed for Rome as a prisoner. Because sailing had been rough, Paul advised his guard that it wouldn't be a good idea to continue the journey. However, they sailed on, ran into a storm, and were shipwrecked on the shore of Malta. Idea 4, "Shipwrecked," will show students that God can use difficulties to bring people close to him.

**5.** While shipwrecked on the island of Malta, Paul was bitten by a poisonous snake. When Paul didn't die, the people around saw God's power in action! With Idea 5, "Sweet Serpents," kids will see that God can protect them from anything.

# 1. The Color Purple

*Kids will spray color on cloth to dye it purple.*

**Theme:** God chooses people from all walks of life.

**Scripture Spotlight 1:** "One of the listeners was a woman named Lydia from the city of Thyatira whose job was selling purple cloth. She worshiped God, and he opened her mind to pay attention to what Paul was saying" (Acts 16:14).

**Scripture Spotlight 2:** "They were throwing a net into the lake because they were fishermen. Jesus said, 'Come follow me, and I will make you fish for people' " (Matthew 4:18b-19).

**Collect:** Red and blue pre-mixed fabric dye (such as Rit), two spray bottles (clean, empty detergent sprayers will do), water, old oversized shirts, permanent markers, a clothesline, clothespins, newspaper, plastic bags, and clean white 12-inch squares of cloth such as old sheets or pillowcases or inexpensive muslin

## Here's What to Do:

Before class, pour one ounce of the red fabric dye into one spray bottle and one ounce of the blue fabric dye into the other. Then add three ounces of warm water to each bottle, cap them, and shake them to mix the water with the dye. Warn kids that the dye will stain their clothes so it's important to keep the lids tight and to spray away from others. Set up the clothesline outside and place plenty of newspaper underneath it.

Give each child a 12-inch square of cloth, a permanent marker, and two clothespins. Have kids write their initials on a corner of the cloth. Then have kids line up in pairs, facing the clothesline. Show the first pair how to fasten their cloth squares side by side on the clothesline then put on the old oversized shirts to protect their clothes. Give one partner the spray bottle with the blue dye and the other partner the one with the red dye. Have kids stand about three feet from the clothesline. Explain that partners will have 30 seconds to spray the cloth, being sure to spray both squares equally so the colors will mix to create the color purple. You may have partners spray their own cloth for 15 seconds then switch bottles and continue for another 15 seconds. After partners have sprayed their pieces of cloth, allow the cloth to drip for a bit before you carefully move it to one end of the clothesline.

When everyone has finished, put the materials away and allow the squares to dry completely. Place each piece of cloth in a plastic bag and instruct kids to go home and rinse them several times in cold water then put them in the dryer to seal in the color. The cloth squares can be used as headbands, handkerchiefs, or hairbows when they dry.

## For Further Fun:

● Kids can wad up their fabric, wrap it with rubber bands, and spray it with red and blue dye. After the dye dries, have kids cut off the rubber bands to reveal interesting purple patterns.

● Provide pre-washed white T-shirts, rather than cloth squares, for kids to spray. Kids can sprinkle salt on the wet shirts for a special effect.

# 2. Under the Big Top

*Groups will work together to create indoor tents.*

**Theme:** God uses all of our talents to draw others to himself.

**Scripture Spotlight 1:** "Paul went to visit Aquila and Priscilla. Because they were tentmakers, just as he was, he stayed with them and worked with them" (Acts 18:2b-3).

**Scripture Spotlight 2:** "There are different ways to serve but the same Lord to serve" (1 Corinthians 12:5).

**Collect:** Old bedsheets (available at most thrift stores), markers, a plastic tarp, and thumbtacks

## Here's What to Do:

Form groups of eight and give each group an old bedsheet and several markers. If you do this indoors, spread the sheets over a plastic tarp. Explain that Paul told people about Jesus while he was working as a tent maker. Tell children that God can use their talents, too, to share the good news of his love. Have them decorate the sheets with their talents by writing their names then drawing or writing about all the things they enjoy doing or do well.

As kids work, help them think of their gifts and talents. Encourage students to make their sheets colorful and decorative. After about five minutes, have kids stop working. Help children work together to thumbtack each sheet to the ceiling. You'll need one thumbtack at each corner and a couple in the middle of each sheet. Parts of each sheet should dip down a little. This gives the effect of being inside a Bedouin tent. Have kids lie under their tent ceiling and look at all the talents represented in their class.

## For Further Fun:

● Have the whole class work on one sheet, then tack it up in a corner of the room. Set aside that corner as a special place of affirmation or prayer.

● Instruct each foursome to drape its sheet over several chairs to form a small tent or fort. Kids can stay in their tents while they enjoy a snack, read stories about Paul, or pray together.

# 3. Mapping out Adventure

*Kids will turn folded maps into boats.*

**Theme:** Everyone in the world needs to know about Jesus.

**Scripture Spotlight 1:** "Go! I have chosen Saul for an important work. He must tell about me to those who are not Jews, to kings, and to the people of Israel" (Acts 9:15b).

**Scripture Spotlight 2:** "So go and make followers of all people in the world" (Matthew 28:19a).

**Collect:** Old maps or atlases

## Here's What to Do:

You'll need to guide students through the steps to make this origami boat. As you demonstrate the process, be sure to take time to help and affirm students. You may want to pair up older and younger kids so older ones can help their younger partners.

Give each student an 8½x11-inch piece of an old map or atlas. Then take kids through the following steps to make boats.

- Fold the paper in half horizontally so the map print is on the inside. Fold this new rectangle in half vertically then unfold it.
- With the fold on top, fold the top right corner down and in so it lines up with the crease down the middle. Do the same with the top left corner so you're left with an arrow pointing up.
- Keeping the paper folded, grasp the top layer of the bottom edge and crease it up. Turn your paper over and do the same with the other side. This shape may look like a boat (or a hat) but you're not finished yet!
- Place your thumbs in the middle of the "hat" as if you're going to put it on your head. Pull outward, then flatten the sides of the hat. You should have a diamond shape that's open at the bottom.
- Bring the bottom of the diamond up to the top, then crease. Turn it over and repeat on the other side.
- Again, place your thumbs inside the bottom of the triangle and pull out. Flatten your new diamond shape.
- Grasp the top points of the diamond on either side of the "seam" and gently pull. Flatten your new shape, and you'll have a boat!

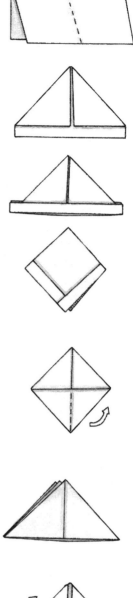

## For Further Fun:

- Tape a large map of the world onto a wall. Have kids pin their boats to different countries then agree to pray for people in those countries every day for a week.
- Kids can write out Matthew 28:18 on their boats and put them on mirrors as reminders to tell others about Jesus.

# 4. ShipWrecked

*Kids in an assembly line will create peanut-butter-banana boats.*

**Theme:** God uses difficult situations for good.

**Scripture Spotlight 1:** "The angel said, 'Paul, do not be afraid. You must stand before Caesar. And God has promised you that he will save the lives of everyone sailing with you.' So men, have courage" (Acts 27:24-25a).

**Scripture Spotlight 2:** "We went through fire and flood, but you brought us to a place with good things" (Psalm 66:12b).

**Collect:** One banana per student, paper plates, plastic knives, and peanut butter (optional: roasted peanuts and chocolate syrup)

## Here's What to Do:

Have kids wash their hands, then form groups of three. Instruct each child to choose one of the following roles: boat peeler, boat splitter, or boat filler. Explain that the boat peeler will peel the bananas and set each one on a paper plate, the boat splitter will cut each banana down the middle, and the boat filler will spread peanut butter on one half of each banana and place the halves back together. You may have kids "storm" their banana boats with chocolate syrup and roasted peanuts as a finishing touch. Then have each trio serve its banana boats to another trio.

## For Further Fun:

● Have kids write on slips of paper things they're thankful for, then spear the slips of paper with toothpicks. Kids can stick the toothpicks in the banana boats as masts and sails.

● As kids eat their boats, have them talk about how God has helped them through hard times.

# 5. Sweet Serpents

*Kids will have fun making candy snakes.*

**Theme:** God protects us from danger.

**Scripture Spotlight 1:** "A poisonous snake came out because of the heat and bit him on the hand...But Paul shook the snake off into the fire and was not hurt" (Acts 28:3, 5).

**Scripture Spotlight 2:** "But the Lord is faithful and will give you strength and will protect you from the Evil One" (2 Thessalonians 3:3).

**Collect:** Tissue paper, a ruler, scissors, colored fruit rings cereal, individually wrapped hard candies, and transparent tape

## Here's What to Do:

Give each child a 2×24-inch rectangle of tissue paper, a handful of fruit rings cereal, transparent tape, and a handful of wrapped hard candies. Show kids how to fold their tissue paper in half the long way then open it and fold the edges so they meet at the center fold. Tape the edges together to form a long tube, then tape one end closed.

Instruct each student to drop one of the candies into the sleeve and slide it to the taped end. Then demonstrate how to *gently* push the tissue paper through the hole in a piece of colored fruit rings cereal and slide the fruit ring until it rests against the hard candy. Have each child drop another piece of candy down the paper sleeve and secure it with a fruit ring. Remind kids to work slowly, being careful not to tear their paper. Allow kids to continue until their snakes are full. Then help students tape off the open ends.

## For Further Fun:

● Kids may want to decorate their tissue paper before creating snakes. Have them drop different colors of watercolor paint onto the paper to get a soft, blended effect!

● This activity can also be done with colored cellophane so the candies show through. Instead of using fruit ring cereal, kids can tie pieces of colored yarn between the pieces of candy.